MW01181396

IMAGES
*of America*

# EUCLID GOLF
# NEIGHBORHOOD

# EUCLID GOLF ALLOTMENT

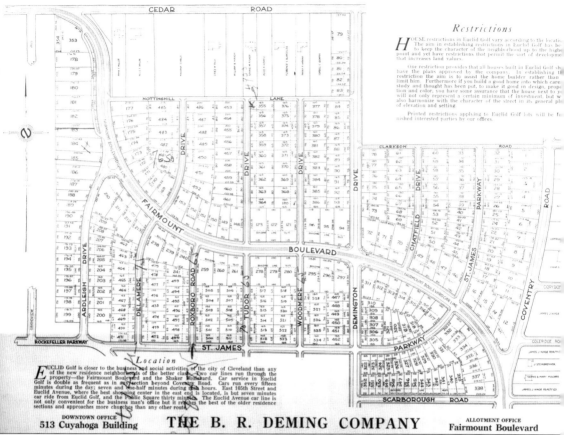

*Location*

EUCLID Golf is closer to the business and social activities of the city of Cleveland than any of the new residence neighborhoods of the better class. Two car lines run through the property—the Fairmount Boulevard and the Shaker Boulevard. Car service in Euclid Golf is double as frequent as in any section beyond Coventry Road. Cars run every fifteen minutes during the day; seven and one-half minutes during rush hours. East 105th Street and Euclid Avenue, where the best shopping center in the east end is located, is but seven minutes car ride from Euclid Golf, and the Public Square thirty minutes. The Euclid Avenue car line is not only convenient for the business man's office but it reaches the best of the older residence sections and approaches more churches than any other route.

**DOWNTOWN OFFICE** 513 Cuyahoga Building     **THE B. R. DEMING COMPANY**     **ALLOTMENT OFFICE** Fairmount Boulevard

This street map of the Euclid Golf Allotment appears in the B.R. Deming Company sales brochure published *c.* 1916. Lots are numbered beginning from the corner of Coventry and Clarkson Roads. Large lots front Fairmount Boulevard, while smaller ones line the side streets. Owners of the houses surrounding Euclid Golf are shown on the map, but are not actually part of Euclid Golf. Note the existence of Upper Drive where Fairmount Boulevard meets Cedar Road and how Nottinghill Lane was planned to go through to Fairmount Boulevard. (The Western Reserve Historical Society, Cleveland, Ohio.)

IMAGES
*of America*

# EUCLID GOLF
# NEIGHBORHOOD

Deanna L. Bremer and Hugh P. Fisher

ARCADIA

Published by Arcadia Publishing,
an imprint of Tempus Publishing, Inc.
Charleston SC, Chicago, Portsmouth NH,
San Francisco

Printed in Great Britain.

Library of Congress Catalog Card Number: 2004100626

For all general information contact Arcadia Publishing at:
Telephone 843-853-2070
Fax 843-853-0044
E-Mail sales@arcadiapublishing.com
For customer service and orders:
Toll-Free 1-888-313-2665

Visit us on the internet at http://www.arcadiapublishing.com

# CONTENTS

| | | |
|---|---|---|
| Acknowledgments | | 6 |
| Photograph Credits | | 6 |
| About the Authors | | 6 |
| Introduction | | 7 |
| 1. | Development of Cleveland's Eastern Suburbs | 9 |
| 2. | Euclid Golf's Developer, Barton R. Deming | 17 |
| 3. | Development of Euclid Golf | 33 |
| 4. | Homes of Euclid Golf | 55 |
| 5. | Prominent People of Euclid Golf | 87 |
| 6. | Marketing Euclid Golf | 95 |
| 7. | Howell & Thomas Architects | 113 |
| Bibliography | | 127 |

# Acknowledgments

The authors wish to thank Stephen Zietz and the staff of the Cleveland Public Library; Anne Sindelar and the staff of the Western Reserve Historical Society; Dr. Darwin Stapleton and the staff of the Rockefeller Archives; Christopher Roy of the Cleveland Heights Historical Society; William Barrow of Cleveland State University; Tom Wolfe, Barbara Powers, and Steve Gordon of the Ohio Historic Preservation Office of the Ohio Historical Society; Frank Quinn of Heritage Ohio and the staffs of the Cuyahoga County Archives, Columbus Metropolitan Library, and Bexley Public Library for their assistance in helping locate source materials and photographs. We would also like to thank Kara Hamley-O'Donnell of the City of Cleveland Heights for her valuable assistance in researching Euclid Golf properties and Mark Genszler and Craig Bobby, for their research assistance. Special thanks to the residents of Euclid Golf, Robert Albrecht, Weston Schmitt, Grant Deming Jr., and members of the Thomas family for sharing with us their photographs and personal recollections of the people who built Euclid Golf. Thanks also to Hugh's mom, Diana Fisher, for her graphic design help; to Deanna's colleague at the Cleveland Restoration Society, E. Michael Fleenor, for his advice; and to Professor Walter Leedy of Cleveland State University for bringing us together.

## Photograph Credits

The sources for the photographs in this book have been identified in each caption. One important contributor of photographs is Mr. Robert S. Albrecht, son of Howell & Thomas designer Herman J. Albrecht. Photographs from Mr. Albrecht's collection have been identified with the abbreviation RSA. Another important contributor of photographs is Mr. Weston Schmitt, the grandson of Barton Deming.

## About the Authors

Authors Deanna Bremer and Hugh Fisher reside in Euclid Golf. The quest to discover their homes' architects led them to seek out the descendents of the people who developed the neighborhood. In talking and meeting with each of these fascinating people, they uncovered hundreds of original advertisements and marketing materials from the B.R. Deming Company, many letters written to John D. Rockefeller's Abeyton Realty Company, several hundred photographs of the neighborhood as it was being developed, and hundreds of Howell & Thomas Architects' original drawings in the Thomas family's attic. Many of these materials have since been donated to the City of Cleveland Heights or the Cleveland Public Library.

Although they had no formal training in historic preservation, what they found compelled them to collaborate on writing the nomination to have Euclid Golf listed in the National Register of Historic Places. Today, Euclid Golf remains much as it was when it was first built. The wonderful mixture of large and small homes, the beautifully curving streets, the quality of materials, and the fine architectural details continue to make Euclid Golf a highly desirable place to live.

# INTRODUCTION

Long before the phrase "golf course community" became synonymous with high-quality residential development, one of the finest neighborhoods in the country rose upon the site of a golf course. Built on land owned by John D. Rockefeller and loaned to the Euclid Club for its golf grounds, the Euclid Golf Neighborhood is an excellent example of early twentieth century real estate planning.

Developer Barton R. Deming brought together Cleveland's leading architects and builders. He practiced principles of the Garden City movement and closely monitored and improved upon the successes he observed in other Cleveland suburban developments, such as Patrick Calhoun's Euclid Heights and the Van Sweringen brothers' Shaker Village. Deming instituted a series of deed restrictions designed to control the quality of the development and thereby protect the investments of individual homeowners. The short period of development, 1913–1929 (only four Euclid Golf homes were built between 1930 and 1950, when the deed restrictions were lifted), produced a cohesive neighborhood whose look and feel has remained virtually unchanged to the present day.

Euclid Golf's architect-designed, single-family homes were built with high quality materials and excellent craftsmanship. Many of the homes were designed by the leading Cleveland-area architects of the time, including Howell & Thomas, Meade & Hamilton, Maxwell Norcross, Charles Schneider, and Walker & Weeks. The homes were designed in a wide variety of styles that represent the evolving domestic architecture of the time. Those built from 1913–1919 tend to be more eclectic and overtly American, such as Shingle and Prairie Style, while those built after World War I tend to be European Revival styles.

Euclid Golf typifies early twentieth century suburbanization in Cleveland. During the late 1800s, Cleveland's iron and steel industries grew dramatically. Large numbers of immigrants were drawn to Cleveland by the relatively abundant low-skilled jobs that these industries offered. As the city's population grew, it crowded into existing neighborhoods adjacent to the factories and transportation lines. Industrialization in the late 1800s produced increased noise, crowding, and pollution. Commercial interests began to encroach upon the wealthy neighborhoods surrounding world famous Euclid Avenue, and citizens of those neighborhoods began to desire a more spacious, healthful environment in which to live.

Cleveland's suburbanization occurred earlier and more rapidly than in other American cities, and Cleveland's elite pioneered its suburban expansion, especially to the east. In 1900, 10 percent of Cleveland's elite already lived in suburban locations. By 1915, the figure had grown to 34 percent. By 1931, 82 percent of Cleveland's wealthiest citizens lived in the suburbs. Cleveland Heights was one of the first centers of elite suburban growth. In 1900, 1.5 percent of Cleveland's elite lived in what would become Cleveland Heights. By 1915, the figure was 9 percent, and in 1931, 35 percent of Cleveland's elite made their homes in Cleveland Heights.

The fear of losing a home and neighborhood to encroaching industrialization was very real to potential homebuyers in Euclid Golf. Depreciation, rather than appreciation, was the norm for residential real estate. Deed restrictions, such as those instituted by the B.R. Deming Company, were the only protection before the advent of zoning. In Euclid Golf, Garden City design principles, the incorporation of the beauty of the natural environment, the use of architects to design beautiful homes, and carefully defined investment levels were used to create a suburban community that would hold its value over time.

This unique neighborhood's history and development has been carefully documented in this book. Hundreds of photographs of the area being developed, marketing brochures, original advertisements, and Howell & Thomas Architects' original drawings have been uncovered and assembled by the authors to tell the story of Euclid Golf, which was listed in the National Register of Historic Places in 2002.

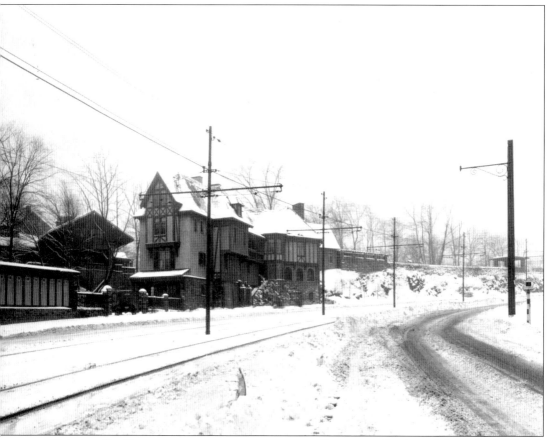

This is a familiar scene to anyone turning onto Fairmount Boulevard from Cedar Road. Perched on the edge of a cliff is the house of Barton R. Deming, the developer of Euclid Golf. Today, Deming's house looks just as it did in this photograph taken in the winter of 1919. Missing today is the additional garage in the foreground, as well as the house of Deming's neighbor P.W. Miller. (RSA.)

# One

# DEVELOPMENT OF CLEVELAND'S
# EASTERN SUBURBS

As commerce and urbanization encroached upon the once tranquil Euclid Avenue, known as "Millionaires' Row," Cleveland's elite sought to escape the noise and grime. The advent of the electric street railway in the 1890s provided the means to climb to the more peaceful, healthful "Heights." Although only six miles from downtown Cleveland, mid-nineteenth century Cleveland Heights was primarily farmland, quarries, and vineyards. The land that would become Euclid Golf was a timber farm.

In 1890, Patrick Calhoun, a prominent lawyer and grandson of Vice President John C. Calhoun, began planning Euclid Heights on 300 acres of land on top of Cedar Hill. He called it "Euclid" after the grand avenue where Cleveland's most prominant citizen's lived; "Heights" described its lofty and healthful location. Landscape architect E.W. Bowditch laid it out on the "Garden City" model, planting abundant trees along gently curving streets. Calhoun's Euclid Heights Realty Company instituted deed restrictions, controlling lot size and minimum home costs. Commercial uses were also prohibited. In 1896, the Cleveland Electric Railway Company brought a streetcar franchise up Cedar Hill to help make Calhoun's vision a reality.

Meanwhile, the Garden City Movement was taking hold in Cleveland. By the 1890s, Cleveland's leadership sought relief from overcrowding and pollution through the organization of a park system. The Shaker Heights Land Company, predecessors of the Van Sweringens, purchased a large tract of land from the defunct Shaker settlement in 1899 and took advantage of the new emphasis on green space to enhance the salability of their land in the Heights. They donated land along Doan Brook and convinced the Amblers, Calhoun, and Rockefeller to do likewise, creating parkland and roads (North Park, South Park, and East Boulevard) to connect the Heights to Wade Park, Rockefeller Park, Gordon Park, and Lake Erie below. Their foresight increased the land value adjacent to the parkland and enabled its development into elite neighborhoods.

To further attract elite Clevelanders, Calhoun opened a first-class recreational facility in 1901, the Euclid Club, featuring Cleveland's first professionally designed 18-hole golf course. Architects Meade & Garfield designed the English style clubhouse, and golf pro William Herbert (Bertie) Way laid out the course. Upon discovering he did not have enough land for a proper 18-hole course, Calhoun made an agreement with neighboring property owner, John D. Rockefeller Sr., who agreed to lease his property to the club rent free with the stipulation that golf not be played on the Sabbath. The course was then laid out so that the ninth and eighteenth greens came up to the clubhouse. On Sundays, members played the lower holes twice.

In 1906, Rockefeller permitted the Cleveland Street Railroad Company to run a line through his property connecting the Cedar Road line to Coventry Road. With the increasing availability of transportation, many homes were springing up in the Heights. Calhoun's Euclid Heights lay to the north, M.M. Brown's Mayfield Heights and Grant Deming's Forest Hill just east of that, and Ambler Heights to the west. Earlier, in 1904, the Shaker Heights Land Company planned to subdivide and develop land on the eastern edge of the lower Euclid Club golf links that ran through Rockefeller's land and produced an elaborate brochure to market the property. However, the company went bankrupt, and the plan was never completed. In 1907, the Van Sweringen brothers took up where they left off and developed a section east of Rockefeller's land. Homes now surrounded the Euclid Club.

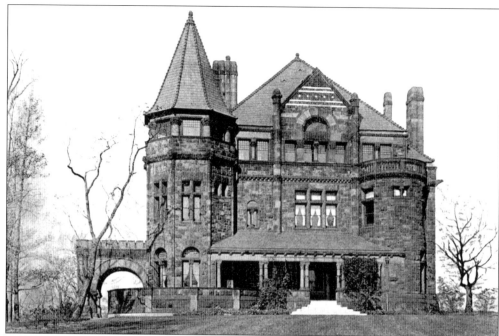

Sylvester T. Everett's Euclid Avenue home appeared in *Beautiful Homes of Cleveland* published in 1917. Everett's house, built from 1883–1887, typifies the street's grandeur. Everett lured Charles F. Schweinfurth (and his brother Julius) from Boston to design his 20,000-square-foot, Romanesque mansion, and many other Euclid Avenue denizens soon followed suit. Schweinfurth's last commission was likely 2504 Fairmount Boulevard in Euclid Golf, built by and for J. Wentworth Smith. (Author Collection.)

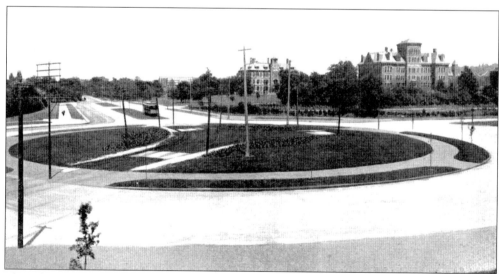

The sales brochure produced for the Shaker Heights Land Company by marketer O.C. Ringle promoted the accessibility of the Heights via streetcar transportation. This view from the brochure shows University Circle at Euclid Avenue near East 107th Street. While University Circle now refers to the cultural center of Cleveland it was originally a traffic circle and streetcar turnaround. (Author Collection.)

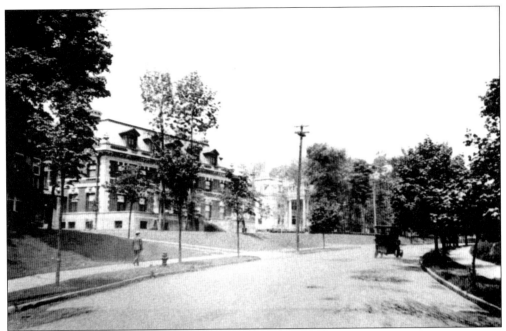

A view from Overlook Road on the edge of Patrick Calhoun's Euclid Heights c. 1910 shows the elaborate mansions that lined the streets. Although these homes were far more modern than those their owners had vacated on Euclid Avenue, most of them also fell to the wrecking ball due to the difficulty of maintaining such large estates during leaner times. (Christopher Roy.)

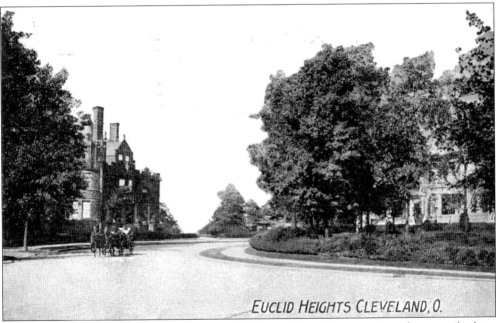

EUCLID HEIGHTS CLEVELAND, O.

This turn of the twentieth century postcard depicts a few of the mansions that were built in Patrick Calhoun's Euclid Heights Allotment. The grand stone mansions, which mimicked those on Euclid Avenue, were set on large lots along wide curving boulevards that bore English names, such as Derbyshire, Hampshire, and Kenilworth. (City of Cleveland Heights.)

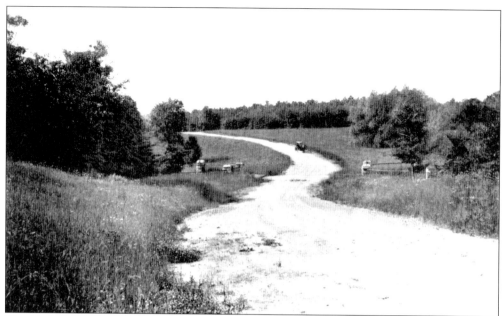

The Shakers had owned land in the "Heights" since 1822. Soon after the Shaker community dissolved in 1889, their land was sold to a group of investors called the Shaker Heights Land Company. They laid out streets and building lots aimed at upscale buyers. The land was marketed by the O.C. Ringle Company, which published an extensive brochure. This c. 1904 photograph from the Ringle brochure shows the rural Shaker landscape that was soon to be developed. (Author Collection.)

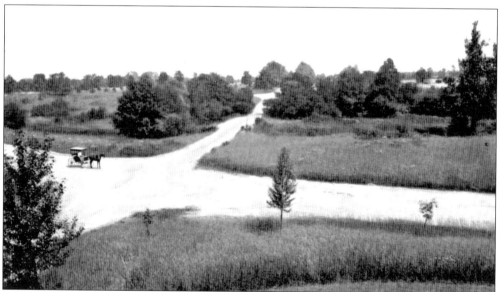

Another view of Shaker land shows a rugged landscape. Although real estate marketers O.C. Ringle billed the Shaker Heights Land Company property as "advantageously situated" at the top of Cleveland's newly created park system, the hilltop paradise was out of reach for most Clevelanders, the majority of whom did not own private automobiles. In 1906, the Van Sweringen brothers took over the property and marketed the lots as Shaker Village. (Author Collection.)

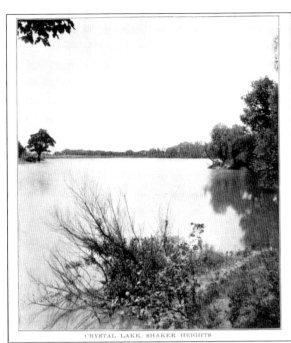

# Shaker Heights

### IDEAL HOME SITES

*Pure Air and Water*

### COUNTRY SURROUNDINGS
### CITY CONVENIENCES

*Best Values in Suburban Property*

## O. C. RINGLE & CO.

*Sole Agents*

401-404 Society for Savings

CLEVELAND

TELEPHONES :
Bell, Main 1578
Cuy., Central 1514

CRYSTAL LAKE, SHAKER HEIGHTS

The frontispiece of the elaborate O.C. Ringle & Company sales brochure promotes Shaker Heights as an ideal location for Clevelanders seeking to escape the dirt and noise of the city. Residents would enjoy fresh air, recreation on the Shaker Lakes, and proximity to the newly created Euclid Club and its 18-hole golf course. The financial depression of the 1890s dampened the success of this venture, and few lots were sold. (Author Collection.)

*T*HE only obstacle in the past preventing the rapid development and settlement of this territory, has been lack of transportation facilities. This difficulty has now been entirely overcome, for recently rights of way have been secured, and franchises granted for a street railroad through this property from Cedar road to Warrensville. A company has been organized and is known as The Shaker Lakes & Boulevard Electric Railway Company. Work upon the construction of the road will be commenced at once. Cars will be run over the lines of the Cleveland Electric railway from the Public Square out Euclid avenue to Fairmount street, thence through Cedar Glens to the city limits.

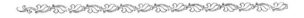

Despite O.C. Ringle's heavy promotion, it was the Van Sweringen brothers who in 1906 finally persuaded the Cleveland Electric Railway to extend their Cedar Hill line to Fairmount Boulevard. To do so they also had to negotiate agreements with Patrick Calhoun because the tracks would pass through the upper nine holes of his Euclid Club's golf grounds and with John D. Rockefeller because he owned the land on which the upper nine lay. (Author Collection.)

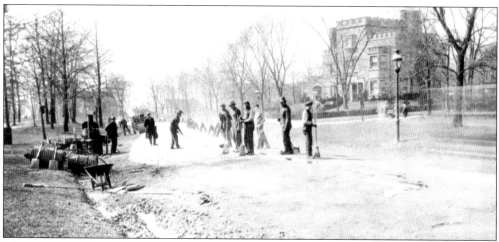

This c. 1910s photograph shows a crew working on the still muddy North Park Boulevard. North Park lies just south of Euclid Golf. The stone Tudor Revival townhouse in the background was built by and for J. Wentworth Smith, master stonemason for Euclid Avenue architect Charles Schweinfurth and president of Fairmount Tool & Forging. Smith would later build a house for himself on Fairmount Boulevard in Euclid Golf. (Christopher Roy.)

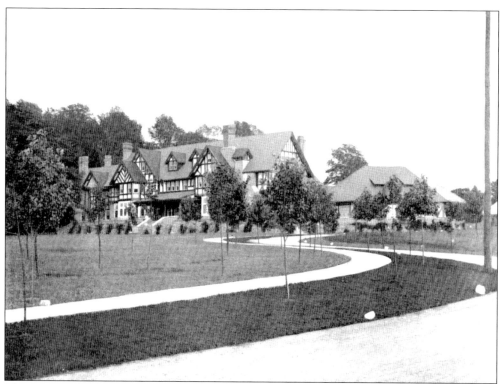

This picture shows the Euclid Golf Club House, designed by the firm Meade & Garfield and completed in 1901. Architect Charles Schneider, who would later go on to design Stan Hywet Hall in Akron, worked for the firm and signed the original rendering of the clubhouse. Frank Meade would later form the illustrious residential architecture firm Meade & Hamilton. Abram Garfield was the late president's son. (Author Collection.)

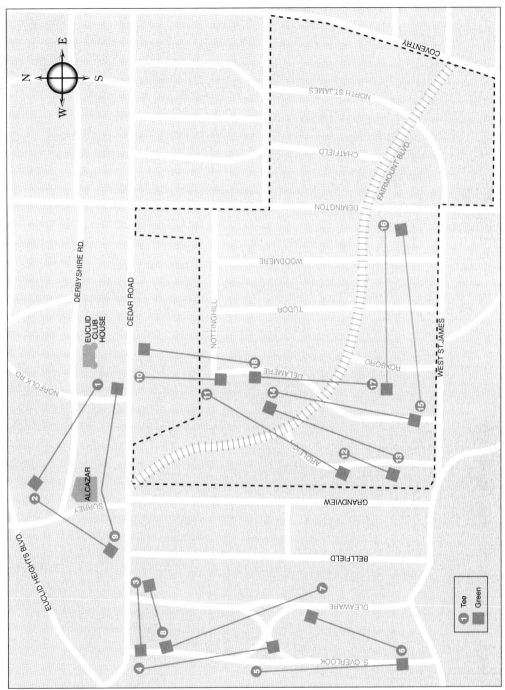

A map of the Euclid Club grounds appeared in the *Plain Dealer* when the club opened. The authors have added a current street map to show the approximate location of the 18 holes. Golfers teed off at the clubhouse, crossed Cedar, and returned to the clubhouse to finish nine. The 10th through 18th holes were across Cedar on the grounds that would become the Euclid Golf Allotment. The dotted line represents Euclid Golf's boundaries. (Thanks to William Barrow for sourcing the original links layout; map graphic by Diana Fisher.)

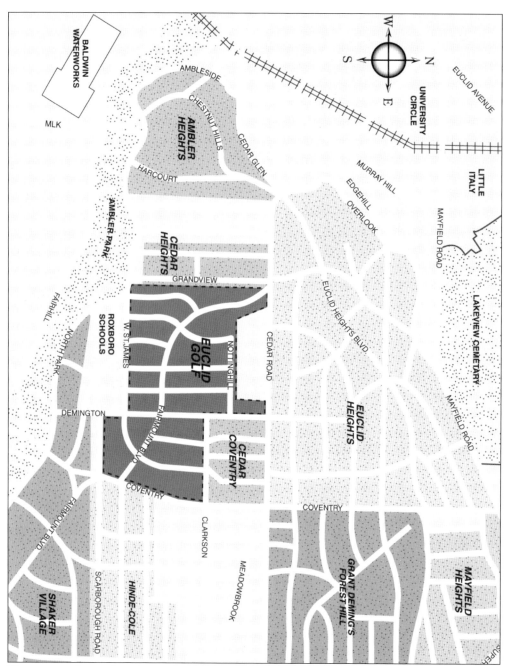

This map, drawn by the authors, shows Euclid Golf and the surrounding residential developments c. 1913. Calhoun's Euclid Heights lay to the north. East of Coventry Road lay Marcus Brown's Mayfield Heights and Barton Deming's brother Grant's Forest Hill Allotment (which had also been Rockefeller land). The Cedar-Coventry Allotment was laid out in the 1910s on the Harbaugh estate. To the west, the Walton brothers developed Cedar Heights in the 1890s, and the Amblers developed Ambler Heights in 1906. The Van Sweringen's original Shaker Village was along Fairmount largely east of Coventry. Their later Shaker Heights development, established in 1912, lay to the southeast. (Map graphic by Diana Fisher.)

## Two
# EUCLID GOLF'S DEVELOPER,
# BARTON R. DEMING

Barton Roy Deming was born in Windsor, Canada, August 21, 1875. His father, Hubert Vilender Deming, was originally from Watertown, New York, and he settled in Canada in the mercantile and lumber business. The ninth of ten children, Deming was educated in Sarnia, Canada, and graduated from its high school in 1892. He followed several of his brothers to Cleveland, Ohio, in 1893.

In Cleveland, Deming worked in the ordering department for the Mechanical Rubber Company and then as a bookkeeper for Oglebay, Norton & Company. Following two years in the West to improve his health, he rejoined his brothers in 1903 to organize the Deming Brothers Company, a real estate concern. Hubert V. Deming Jr., the oldest brother, was president of the firm; Grant was vice-president and manager; Orville was secretary; and Barton was treasurer. Cecil, the youngest brother, was also involved.

The Demings developed several high-quality allotments in East Cleveland such as the Grantwood and Columbia Allotments. Cleveland historian, Samuel Orth, wrote in 1910: "The real-estate operations of the firm have constituted an important chapter in the history of Cleveland for the past six years, the development, upbuilding and adornment of the city being largely promoted through their efforts. They have opened up many of the finest additions in Cleveland and have erected residence property of the highest grade."

In 1905, Grant Deming organized the Deming Realty Company. This company developed the Hyde Park Allotment in Cleveland Heights. In 1909, Grant's Heights Realty, Cleveland Heights Realty, and Boulevard Land & Building Company developed the Forest Hill Allotment on land previously owned by John D. Rockefeller (roughly bounded by Euclid Heights to the north, Coventry Road to the west, Lee Road and Superior Street to the east, and Cedar Road to the south), also in Cleveland Heights.

Barton Deming split from his brothers to form the B.R. Deming Company in order to develop Rockefeller's Euclid Golf property. He built his home in 1914 on a sliver of land where Fairmount Boulevard intersects with Cedar Road. It served as a unique advertisement and a gateway to the Euclid Golf Neighborhood. He contracted architects Howell & Thomas to design 2485 Fairmount on a narrow, steep, and rocky site with a deep gorge running through it. Howell & Thomas relished the challenge of building on such a site, and Deming was proud of the resulting four-story French Eclectic mansion. It embodied his aspirations for Euclid Golf.

Deming lived here from 1914 until the death of his wife, Helen, in March of 1934 and the marriage of his only daughter, Elaine Allen, to Weston Schmitt the same year. His nephew, Grant Deming Jr., helped him auction off his furnishings and then lived with him in the Heights Rockefeller Building apartments at Mayfield and Lee roads in Cleveland Heights. Deming then worked for John D. Rockefeller Jr. to develop Rockefeller Sr.'s Forest Hill estate into the residential village that straddles the East Cleveland and Cleveland Heights border today. When Cleveland Heights established a Zoning Commission in 1920, Deming was one of its first appointed members.

Towards the end of his life, Deming lived with his sister Millie on Stoer Road in Shaker Heights. He served for many years as a trustee of the Cleveland Real Estate Board and later established the Deming Ironing Company, which manufactured gas electric ironing machines. He died at Overlook House, a Christian Science Home, in Cleveland Heights, on September 15, 1956, at the age of 81.

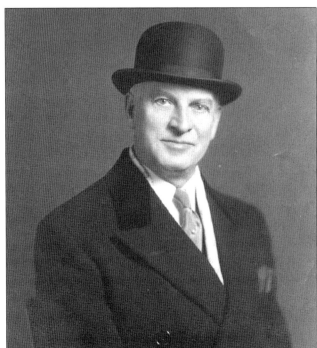

Barton R. Deming was Canadian born and educated. He came to the United States in 1895 when he was 20 and entered real estate in 1904. For many years, he was a trustee of the Cleveland Real Estate Board and the Cleveland Heights Zoning Board. He belonged to the Cleveland Athletic and Shaker Country Clubs and was a 32nd degree Mason. A Christian Scientist, he was a trustee of Overlook House, a retirement home at which he later resided. (Weston Schmitt.)

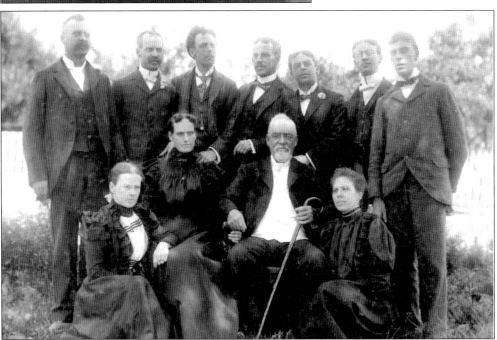

The Deming family at their home in Windsor, Canada, standing from left to right, are: Stark Windle (born 1859), Orville Gurney (1862), Eli Rogers (1865), Hubert Vilender Jr. (1867), Grant Wilson (1872), Barton Roy (1875), and Claire Claiborne (1878); and sitting from left to right are: Lois Hannah (1857), Jennie, Hubert Vilender Sr. (1830), and Millie Eveline (1869). Not pictured is daughter, Nora Irene (1860), and mother, Susan, who passed away in 1879. (Grant Deming Jr.)

John D. Rockefeller Sr. is seen here playing golf *c.* 1910. An avid golfer, Rockefeller had golf links on the grounds of his Forest Hill estate in East Cleveland and his home in Ormond Beach, Florida. Although the location in the photograph is unknown, Rockefeller would have certainly played the Euclid Club's links. Rockefeller is buried in Cleveland Heights at Lakeview Cemetery. (The Western Reserve Historical Society, Cleveland, Ohio.)

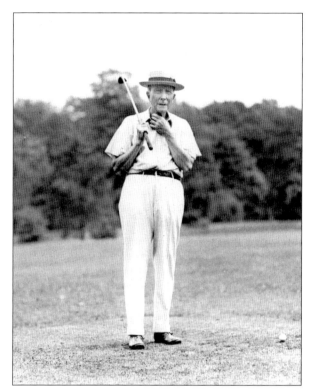

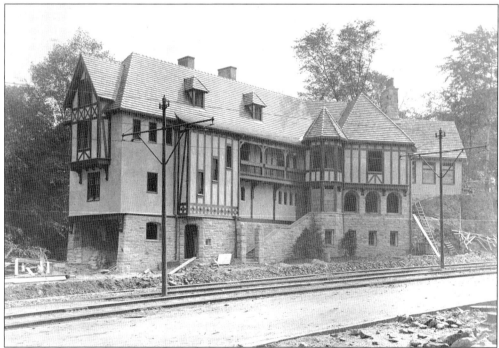

This October 1914 photograph shows Deming's home, 2485 Fairmount, under construction. Its French Eclectic style is particularly suited to the narrow, upward sloping lot. Note the streetcar tracks and construction debris in the foreground. (RSA.)

# THE ABEYTON REALTY CO.

213-215 ROCKEFELLER BUILDING
SUPERIOR AVE. AND WEST SIXTH STREET

CLEVELAND, OHIO  February 5-1913

Business Properties

Acreage for
Allotment

Railroad Frontage

Desirable Lots in
Various Parts of the
City on Easy Terms

Houses, Stores, Suites
for Rent

Dear Mr. Heydt:

Your telegram asking that I forward
the plat of the Cleveland Heights proposed allotment
received, and I am enclosing same.    This is the second
one prepared by Mr. Deming in which I have worked with
him, and one I feel that I can recommend for your con-
sideration, being the most satisfactory, in my judg-
ment,of many that have been prepared from time to time.

This plat makes the minimun frontage for
the side streets  fifty feet, and minimun frontage for
the Boulevard lots sixty feet, both of which will doubtless be sold in larger frontage, but you will note that
the depth in both instances are sufficient for a wider
frontage.   The Boulevard lots averaging over two hundred
feet in depth, and the side streets lots proportionately
deep.    It offers a medium between the large and extravagant allotment, like the Height ( Calhoun) Allotment,
and the smaller and cheaper of the City allotments some
of which are on the Heights.

We have to conform , of course to the established line of the Cleveland Street Railway Company,
which evidently was not taken into account from the allotment standpoint relating to this property.   This makes

In this letter dated February 5, 1913, Clarence E. Terrill, manager of the Abeyton Realty Company, Rockefeller's real estate concern in Cleveland recommended Deming's plan for Euclid Golf. Charles O. Heydt was Rockefeller Sr.'s trusted staffer and real estate advisor. He later became Rockefeller Jr.'s secretary. (The Rockefeller Archive Center.)

# THE ABEYTON REALTY CO.

213-215 ROCKEFELLER BUILDING
SUPERIOR AVE. AND WEST SIXTH STREET

CLEVELAND, OHIO

#2

Business Properties

Acreage for
Allotment

Railroad Frontage

Desirable Lots in
Various Parts of the
City on Easy Terms

Houses, Stores, Suites
for Rent

some irregular shaped lots, which cannot be avoided. The whole plat you will note is carried out independent of the adjoining property making it possible to operate, if necessary without co-operation , and at the same time provides for co-operation along the north line with the property owners for a fifty foot street, if they desire, if not the twenty-five feet shown will make a traffic road, without which there would be dead end streets, but no lots are faced on this thorough-fare. On the south there are streets leading to the Parkway Drive already established on the adjoining property, giving an outlet from the proposed street forming the south line of your property. This plan makes all lots accessable to the street car line on their property as well as your own.

I will enclose a plat of the Hinde-Cole allotment directly opposite of this property on Coventry Road with as many lots as in your tract, which because of the popular size of its lots has had a marvelously ready sale, yet the price has been such as to insure a fine class of houses, which have been building very rapidly. These lots averaged about fifty feet frontage by about one hundred fifty feet deep, as you will note by the plat , few being larger , while your proposed plat calls for larger lots, consequently higher prices. The accessibility to the street cars, and the prox-imity to the City will warrant a higher price, and meet a

One difficulty in developing Euclid Golf was the irregular lot created by the streetcar line that branched off the Cedar Road line and traveled through the property. While most of the other proposals had ignored it, Deming planned to build a gateway house that would catch the eye of prospective buyers. Deming also ensured that his street layout plan could be carried out with or without the cooperation of surrounding property owners. (The Rockefeller Archive Center.)

21

# THE ABEYTON REALTY CO.

213-215 ROCKEFELLER BUILDING
SUPERIOR AVE. AND WEST SIXTH STREET

CLEVELAND, OHIO

#3

**Business Properties**

**Acreage for
Allotment**

**Railroad Frontage**

**Desirable Lots in
Various Parts of the
City on Easy Terms**

**Houses, Stores, Suites
for Rent**

demand for lots ranging in price from fifty to sixty dollars per foot.

This is the only plat with good sized lots that it has been possible to figure out a satisfactory price to the purchaser to warrant the investment. Mr. Deming has surely gone into the matter thoroughly and he has a building organization in connection with his allotment business, and has been very successful, due to some extent in his being able to sell a customer a lot with a house to suit him.

I think, Mr. Deming could handle the proposition along the line suggested in the enclosed plat successfully. There would doubtless be minor changes necessary, but the plat as a whole would remain about as shown here. I will enclose a plat of the Euclid Heights ( Calhoun ) Allotment, which as you know is separated from this plat by Cedar Road and the lots facing Cedar Road, as a matter of comparison. The extravagant and elaborate scheme of this allotment you are more or less familiar with. The over large lots and the price necessary to purchase such lots made the whole proposition impractical. I think the proposed plat,a good medium between this sort of a proposition and the one of to small lots and inexpensive houses, a very practical and

Other developers had proposed developing his property, but Rockefeller ultimately chose Deming's proposal because it offered a happy medium: the lots were not so large that they would be difficult to sell to Cleveland's small upper echelon (as Calhoun, who ultimately went bankrupt, would discover) and not as small as typical city lots. (The Rockefeller Archive Center.)

22

# THE ABEYTON REALTY CO.

213-215 ROCKEFELLER BUILDING
SUPERIOR AVE. AND WEST SIXTH STREET

CLEVELAND, OHIO

#4

Business Properties

Acreage for
Allotment

Railroad Frontage

Desirable Lots in
Various Parts of the
City on Easy Terms

Houses, Stores, Suites
for Rent

salable size lots at a price within the reach of a  man
of ordinary means, who could be interested in and afford
to own a house and lot costing ten thousand dollars. up
This location and the price at which the lots could be sold
would make this possible.  Mr. Deming would surely be a
splendid chap to take hold of it, while his brother Grant
Deming is somewhat discredited, Mr. B. R. Deming stands
high and has no connection in a business way with his
brother Grant. this fact Mr. Deming desired me to state.

Yours very truly,

C. E. Terrill

Mr. Charles O. Heydt,
        26 Broadway,
                New York, N. Y.

The reasons behind Clarence Terrill's comments regarding Barton Deming's brother Grant are unknown. Grant Deming had purchased property from Rockefeller east of Coventry Road in 1906 and had developed a residential allotment he named Forest Hill, referring to Rockefeller's nearby country estate. Grant Deming successfully developed many residential areas in Cleveland Heights and beyond. (The Rockefeller Archive Center.)

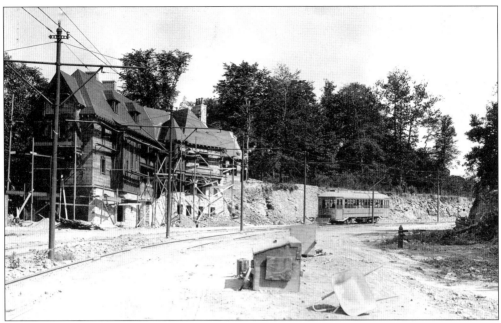

The B.R. Deming Company obtained a building permit for 2485 Fairmount Boulevard on May 4, 1914. This August 1914 photograph shows the house under scaffolding prior to the application of stucco and half timbering. The estimated cost of construction was $6,000. Note the streetcar as it makes its way down the newly created median of Fairmount Boulevard and in the foreground, the tool shed and wheelbarrow on its side (the wheel is nearby). (RSA.)

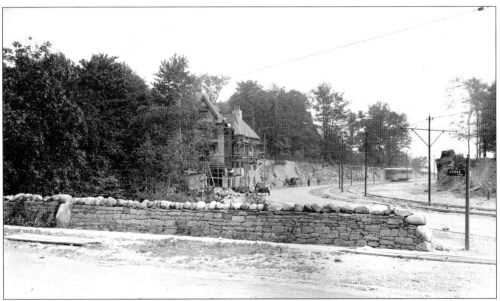

The stone facing for the Deming House and the formidable stone wall that rises along Fairmount Boulevard reportedly was built of sandstone excavated from the construction of the street. The stone wall facing Cedar Road in the foreground of this picture, part of which remains today, likely belongs to the P.W. Miller estate next door to Deming. This photograph is dated August 1914. (RSA.)

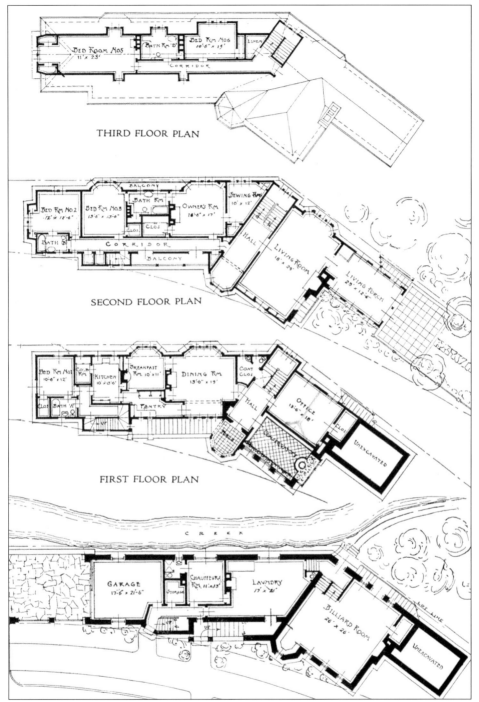

THIRD FLOOR PLAN

SECOND FLOOR PLAN

FIRST FLOOR PLAN

Plans for all four levels of the Deming House were featured in the May 1917 edition of *The Architectural Forum*. The plans show a garage and billiard room on the basement level; an office, kitchen, and dining room on the first floor; a living room and family bedrooms on the second; and servants' rooms on the third. Like a row house, the home is one room wide and several rooms deep. The house is angled to conform to the site.

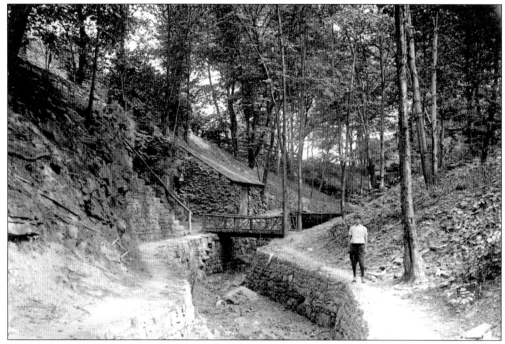

This July 1914 photograph shows the stone retaining walls built to control the creek that runs behind the Deming House. The walls were likely a part of the estate of P.W. Miller, Deming's next door neighbor, whose property included extensive woodland gardens. (RSA.)

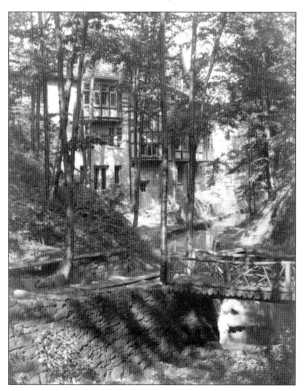

This rear view of the Deming House shows its situation along the creek bed, which forms a deep gorge behind the house. Note the abundance of trees and the rustic wooden bridge that connects both sides of the rear gardens. We believe the bridge pre-dates Deming's house and that it was a part of the Miller estate next door. The photograph is c. 1916. (Weston Schmitt.)

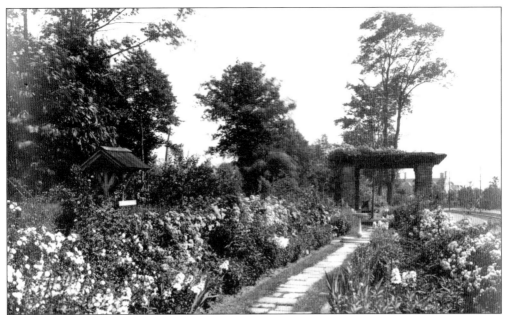

The sunny upper garden of Deming's house shown in this 1920 photograph occupied the sliver of land just above the house along Fairmount Boulevard and exemplifies the desire of suburban planners to combine the convenience of city living with the peacefulness and beauty of the country. The stone and wood pergola exists today. In the distance behind the pergola can be seen the gables and chimneys of the A.C. Ernst residence at Fairmount Boulevard and Ardleigh Drive. (Weston Schmitt.)

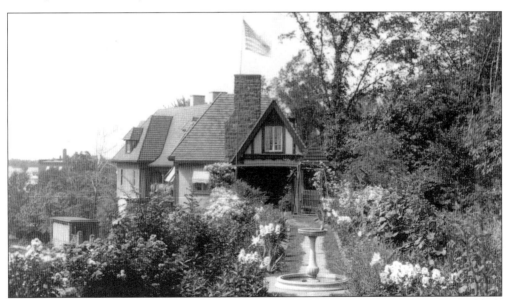

Another view of the upper garden in 1920 shows a flagstone walk, a delicate fountain, and lush plantings. The garden door enters to the second floor living porch, which later became Deming's library. One gets a sense of the grand vistas that can be had from the house, looking down on the City of Cleveland and Lake Erie. A freestanding garage, built in 1916 to supplement the original garage attached to the front of the house, lies in the background. (Weston Schmitt.)

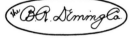

OFFICES AT
FAIRMOUNT BOULEVARD AND
DEMINGTON DRIVE
AND
1110-11-12 WILLIAMSON BLDG.

**QUALITY HOME BUILDERS**
**CLEVELAND**

October 20, 1916.

The Abeyton Realty Company,

26 Broadway,

New York.

Gentlemen:-

We are endeavoring to work out ways and means to promote
sales quickly in Euclid-Golf Allotment, and with this in mind
come always to the same conclusion that activity in building
brings this result most readily.

In opening up the streets south of the Boulevard, as well
as Fairmount itself, we are sure that houses begun on each
street would have a very stimulating effect in every way. As
outlined to you while in New York recently, it takes a great
deal of advance cash to purchase lots outright as well as build
the houses before receiving anything from the investment. Our
competitors to the south, as well as The Van Sweringen Company, are
furnishing lots to builders without advance payment in the following manner: The lot is deeded and a mortgage taken back, made
payable when the house on said lot is completed and sold. An
arrangement of this kind at this time would make it possible for
us to get this new part of the allotment started this fall, and
by spring be in good shape for quick sale, whereas if allowed to

In a letter dated October 20, 1916 written to the Abeyton Realty Company, Barton Deming
requests that Rockefeller finance the construction of eight model homes. The letter, written
on B.R. Deming Company stationery, lists offices at the corner of Fairmount Boulevard and
Demington Drive and at the Williamson Building in downtown Cleveland. (The
Rockefeller Archive Center.)

lay without building activity means much slower development.
We could build about eight houses between now and spring with
this arrangement, which would have a far-reaching effect in
selling lots. We want to build at least two - perhaps more on
the Boulevard - one on Sub-Lot No. 280 - one on Sub-Lot No. 184,
and several on side streets, and make the suggestion that you
deed to us a lot at a time upon a payment of Five Hundred Dollars
($500.00) each for side street lots, and One Thousand Dollars
($1,000) for Boulevard lots, taking back a six percent (6%)
mortgage to be recorded after a bank mortgage for building has
been negotiated, and payable on or before eight months or upon
sale of the property when finished. Our mortgage loans on homes
are never more than fifty percent (50%) of value and the security
is always ample.

 If this plan meets with your approval we would like to begin
at this time on Lot No. 280 Fairmount Boulevard.

 Will be glad to hear from you as soon as possible as the
season is getting late for beginning new building.

                              Very truly yours,

                         THE B. R. DEMING COMPANY

BRD/GEM

*P.S. Copy of above has been given Mr Terrill*

Deming proposed to build at least two model homes on Fairmount Boulevard. Howell & Thomas Architects designed the homes in vastly different styles to demonstrate their capabilities. For 2520 Fairmount (Lot 184) they chose the Adam Colonial Revival style, while 2626 Fairmount (Lot 280) was a half-timbered Tudor Revival. (The Rockefeller Archive Center.)

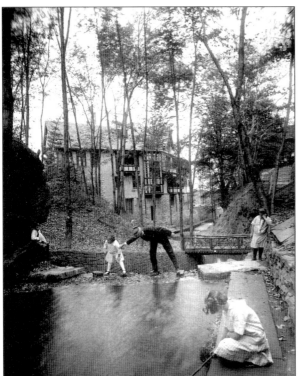

The woodland garden behind Deming's house, shown in a photograph taken in 1917, was complete with waterfall. As mentioned earlier, most of these woodland gardens and waterways were a part of the Miller estate next door. While we do not know the exact identity of the people in the photograph, we presume the gentleman is Deming and that one of the children is his only daughter, Elaine. (Weston Schmitt.)

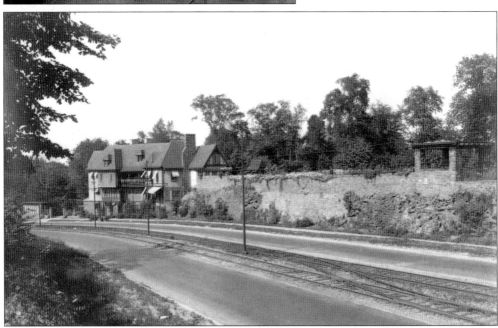

This 1918 photograph is taken from the Upper Drive and shows the length of the Deming house and its gardens. A sandstone wall, created from stone excavated from the Fairmount Boulevard roadbed below, buttresses the sandstone ledge upon which the house was built, adding to the illusion that the house naturally springs from its landscape. A stone pergola marks the end of the rear gardens. (Weston Schmitt.)

A view from a second floor window in the Deming house overlooks the rear garden and the creek below. The skillful siting of the house on its narrow lot created the illusion of secluded country living. Not unlike Frank Lloyd Wright's Falling Water, one is never far removed from the natural landscape. (Weston Schmitt.)

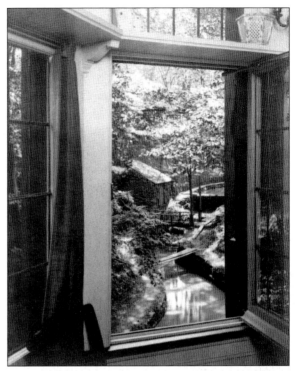

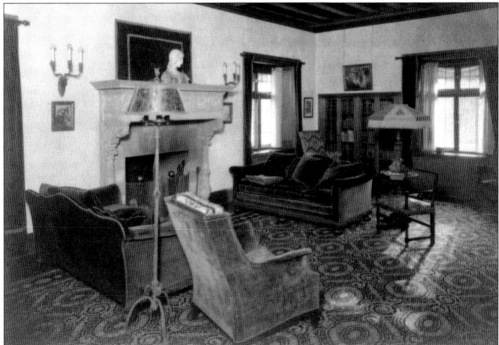

The 12-foot high ceiling in the Deming house living room features birch beams, spaced three feet apart, decorated with Venetian stenciling. Intricate plaster moldings and voluminous windows detailed with leaded glass speak of the home's elegance. An 8-foot tall, white marble rococo fireplace was imported from Italy. (Weston Schmitt.)

26 Broadway
New York

August 26, 1919.

Dear Mr. Rockefeller:

Mr. Deming's contract, which was extended to September 1st, is working out very satisfactorily. Under its terms he was obliged to reduce his indebtedness to $480,000., upon doing which he would be entitled to a deed for the remaining lots and to give you a mortgage on them for the $480,000., payable in three annual installments. Including interest he owes you, as of September 1st, about $466,000., and the remaining lots have a market value of about $750,000., which gives an ample margin over the mortgage.

Thus far Mr. Deming has paid, on principal, $641,645. and in interest $109,740. and you have been relived of all taxes and assments on the property since April 1, 1913. There has not at any time been any income tax on the sales of these lots, for the agreement was entered into and the price of the lots fixed before the Income Tax law went into effect.

We have had to be patient with Mr. Deming on many occasions, but the final result is pleasing and profitable. As against the urgent suggestions of all those who were consulted in the latter part of 1912 and early 1913, that the property be sold for cash, and that you avoid taking part in its development, their figure for the property being $500,000., you agreed to finance the development scheme. You will receive for the land alone $680,000., and be reimbursed for the advances for development, together with interest at 5%. The financing of the development has paid handsomely.

One of the most gratifying features of the enterprise is that real estate men look upon this Euclid Golf Allotment as a model development. Mr. Deming has had many visitors from all parts of the United States inspecting the place, and their universal comment has been that only "Mr. Rockefeller" could do such a fine piece of work. In connection with some inquiries which have been made here by callers I have said that you made your contribution to the housing problem in this development. We could get a lot of advertising out of this if you were inclined to have Mr. Lee write it up.

Very truly,

*Charles O. Heydt*

Mr. John D. Rockefeller, Jr.
Seal Harbor, Maine.

On August 26, 1919, Charles O. Hedyt wrote a letter to his boss, John D. Rockefeller, Sr., discussing the status of the Euclid Golf project. In it he speaks of the financial success of the Euclid Golf Allotment and the acclaim it had received across the country. (The Rockefeller Archive Center.)

# Three
# Development of Euclid Golf

By 1912, the Euclid Golf Club had disbanded and migrated to the Shaker Heights and Mayfield Country Clubs. In addition to encroaching residential development, the members had grown tired of having only nine holes to play on Sunday, their favorite golfing day. In 1913, Barton R. Deming struck a purchase deal with Rockefeller that would enable the 141 acres to be developed into a high-quality residential allotment. Deming would negotiate and oversee all improvements with the approval of Rockefeller's Abeyton Realty Company. Deming relied on Rockefeller's influence and prestige, as well as his bankroll, in gaining the cooperation of the various utility companies, such as the East Ohio Gas Company and the Cleveland Street Railroad Company.

Rockefeller had considered Deming's allotment plan carefully. Others had approached him about developing the upper golf links; however, his Abeyton Realty Company had gained wisdom from both its own ventures and those of other developers. Abeyton believed Calhoun's Euclid Heights' lots were too large and impractical. Deming's proposal contained both large lots (along Fairmount Boulevard) and smaller lots for a more middle class owner. Clarence C. Terrill, Manager of Abeyton, believed Deming's proposal offered a middle ground that would both ensure the profitability of the venture and the neighborhood's design quality.

As Deming set to work developing the allotment, competition from neighboring allotments and Patrick Calhoun's bankruptcy and subsequent sheriff sale of the remaining Euclid Heights property in 1914, negatively affected sales of Euclid Golf. Because his cash flow did not enable him to make timely payments to Rockefeller, and he required additional loans for the necessary property improvements, Deming was forced to renegotiate the terms of his agreement. In 1915, Deming secured an agreement to continue as the sole agent for the development and sale of lots in Euclid Golf until July 31, 1920. Deming paid $89,747 up front, and Abeyton Realty agreed to invest up to $320,000 in physical improvements such as gas, sewers, water, electricity, paving, guttering, and curbing. Abeyton Realty also set a minimum price on the lots thus guaranteeing a minimum payment. When Deming fulfilled all aspects of the contract, he was to be given a warranty deed for the unsold remainder of the property in exchange for a purchase mortgage of $430,000 or the balance of the purchase price then due. Finally, on October 3, 1919, Deming received the mortgage deed for the property for $463,158.40.

We are fortunate that Barton Deming chose to document the construction of the Euclid Golf neighborhood the way he did. Nearly 200 photographs of Euclid Golf in its early years survive (the majority of them are shown in this book). The photographs tell the story of Euclid Golf's development better than any narrative description could. The images of the land as golf links, woods, and orchard show the land as it was prior to residential development. The fact that the streetcar tracks wound through the golf links many years prior to development is strikingly illustrated. Deming documents each road's construction, his billboards and sales offices, and many of the houses that were built in the early years of Euclid Golf's development.

The photographs begin in 1913 and end abruptly in January 1918. We are not sure about the identity of the photographer or even if they were all taken by the same person. One possible photographer is Herman J. Albrecht, the chief designer for Howell & Thomas, who moved from Columbus to Cleveland in 1913 to work in Euclid Golf. He left the firm in 1919 to form his own firm, Albrecht, Wilhelm & Kelly, and took copies of the photographs with him. However, Albrecht never took credit for shooting the photographs. There may have been photographs taken after 1919, but to our knowledge, none of them survive.

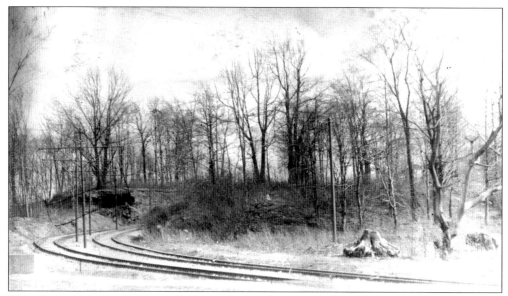

This photograph, dated March 1913, is taken looking south from Cedar Road at what would become the foot of Fairmount Boulevard and the entrance to Euclid Golf. The trolley tracks, in place since 1906, would form the shape of the boulevard. Deming's house would soon dominate the left hand side of the photograph, and by the 1920s, a commercial building would fill the right hand side. (RSA.)

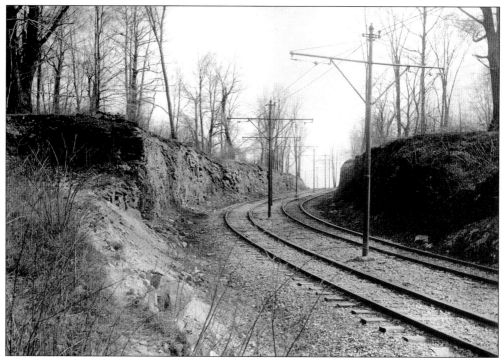

Proceeding a few hundred feet up the tracks from Cedar Road, one can clearly see the excavation required to lay the route for the trolley. These rock outcroppings would soon be removed to make way for Fairmount Boulevard and Deming's house. (RSA.)

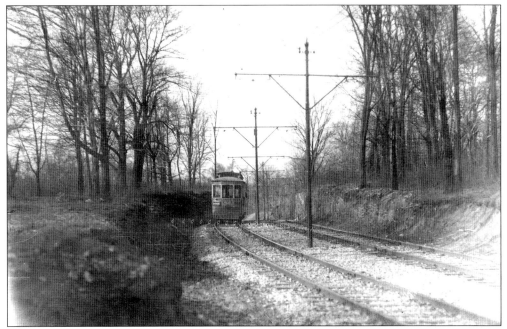

This photograph is taken looking north toward Cedar Road where the tracks come through the rock outcropping. The trolley coming up the hill is eastbound on its way to the Van Sweringen brothers' original Shaker Village development along Fairmount Boulevard east of Coventry Road. (RSA.)

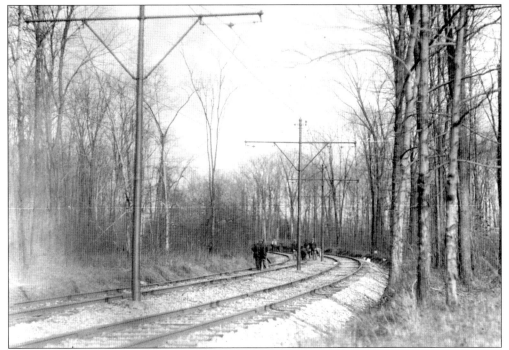

Deming's photographer happened to catch a group of workers making repairs to the trolley tracks in this March 1913 photograph. (RSA.)

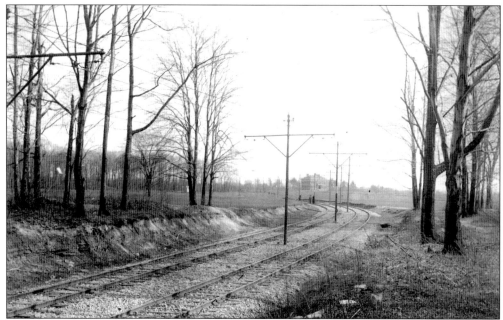

Proceeding a bit further along the trolley tracks, this photograph was taken looking southeast near the point where Ardleigh Drive and Fairmount Boulevard meet today. Emerging from the woods, one can see the golf grounds. Note the people waiting for the trolley, as well as the original Roxboro School building in the distance. The wooded area in the background is where Deming would lay out Tudor and Woodmere Drives. (RSA.)

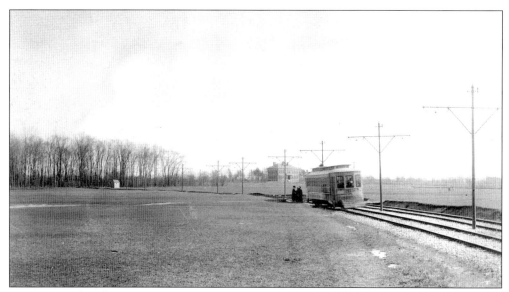

In 1906, Rockefeller permitted the Cleveland Street Railway Company to run a line from Cedar to Coventry Road, directly through the land he leased to the Euclid Club. Taken in 1913 near what would become Fairmount Boulevard and Delamere Drive, the photograph shows the streetcar bisecting the golf grounds at holes 11, 13, 14, and 17. While the streetcar was an inconvenience to the golfers, Rockefeller's prohibition of Sunday golf was more so. In the distance is the original Roxboro Elementary School. (RSA.)

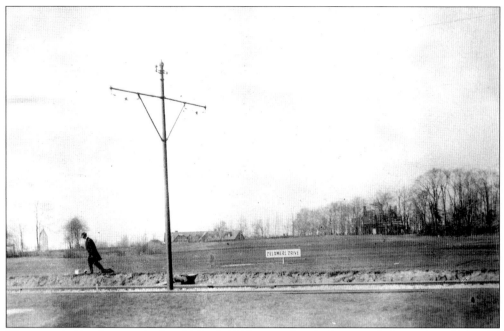

This remarkable photograph, dated March 1913, was taken looking north from where Delamere Drive and Fairmount Boulevard would intersect. In the distance is the roofline of the Euclid clubhouse across Cedar Road. Access to the upper nine was through a clearing between two grand houses that faced Cedar Road, one of which can be seen to the right. Deming, the consummate marketer, had already placed signs to let the streetcar riders know what was to come! (RSA.)

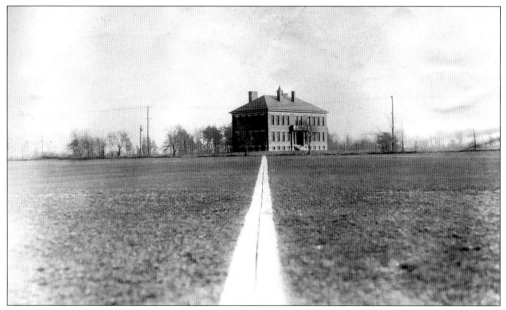

This early 1913 shot shows the original Roxboro School house with the cropped golf course grounds in the foreground. The chalk line is likely the "layout" of the soon to be constructed Roxboro Road, which according to plat maps of the time, heads straight for the corner of the schoolhouse. (RSA.)

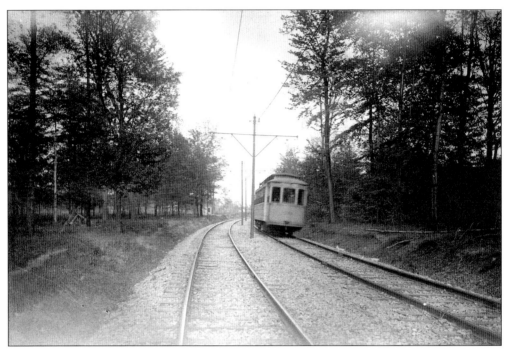

This May 1913 photograph is taken within the wooded section of what would become Fairmount Boulevard. Deming would locate Tudor and Woodmere Drives within this section. (RSA.)

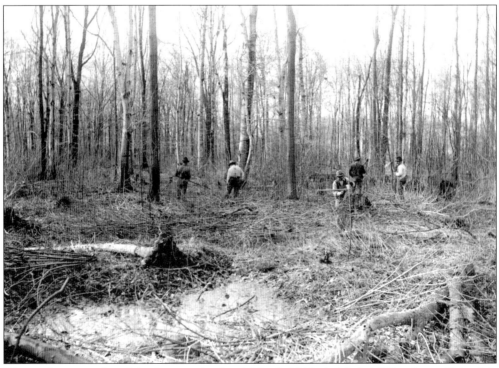

We are fortunate that this photograph, dated March 1913, is labeled "Woodmere Drive." It shows workers beginning to clear access to the wooded lots of Euclid Golf. (RSA.)

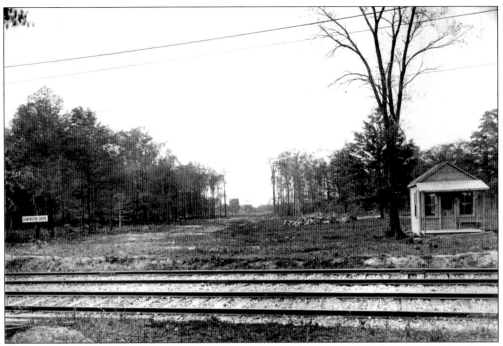

This is the future site of Demington Drive as shown in this May 1913 photograph. The shot is taken looking north from the trolley tracks toward Cedar Road. The building to the right was likely a small shelter in which riders, possibly having walked down a path from Cedar, could wait for the trolley. (RSA.)

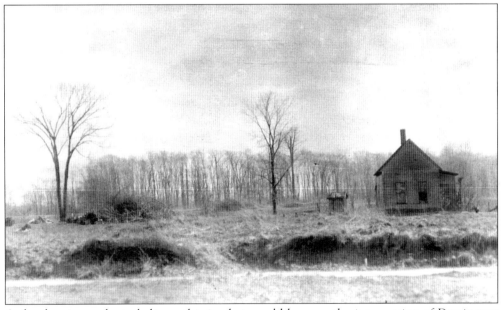

As hard as it may be to believe, this is what would become the intersection of Demington Drive and Cedar Road! This March 1913 photograph was taken looking south from Cedar. The dilapidated shanty complete with outhouse is not representative of Deming's vision for Euclid Golf! (RSA.)

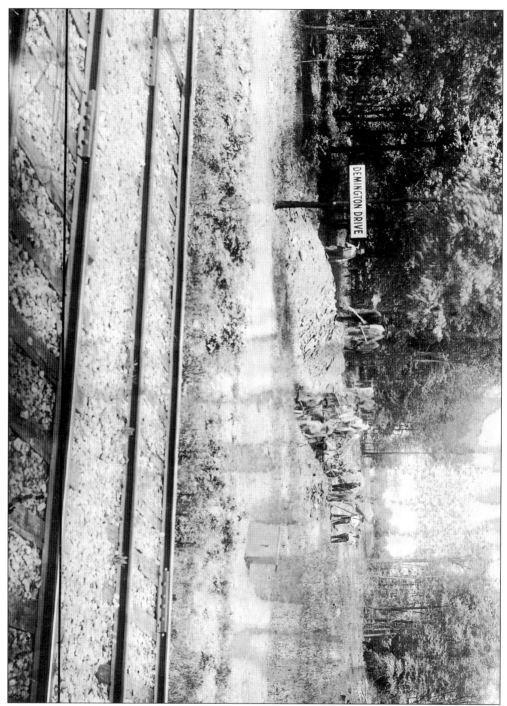

In May 1913, construction on Demington Drive began by hand digging the trench for the drain tile! A careful examination shows that each man digs a bit deeper, resulting in the workers at the end of the line standing up to their shoulders in the trench. Note the surveyor to the right. This shot was taken looking north toward Cedar Road. In the distance is the rear of a shanty and outhouse that faced Cedar. (Weston Schmitt.)

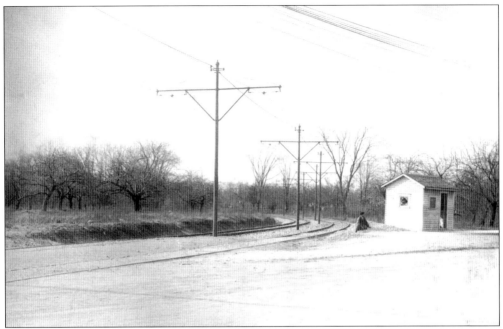

This early 1913 picture shows the Fairmount Line where it crosses Coventry Road on the eastern most border of Euclid Golf. Currently, St. Paul's Church sits to the right. An orchard covered much of the eastern portion of Euclid Golf. Although the small building provided shelter for waiting streetcar passengers, the gent in the picture seems content to wait for his ride sitting upon a pile of gravel. The poles supporting the streetcar's power lines carry streetlights today. (RSA.)

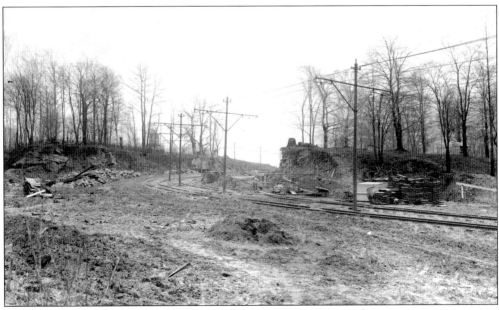

We are back at the beginning of the line at Cedar and Fairmount, with construction progressing with the removal of the stone outcroppings in preparation of building Fairmount Boulevard and Deming's house. Note the steam shovel doing the heavy lifting this time. This photograph was taken in February 1914. (RSA.)

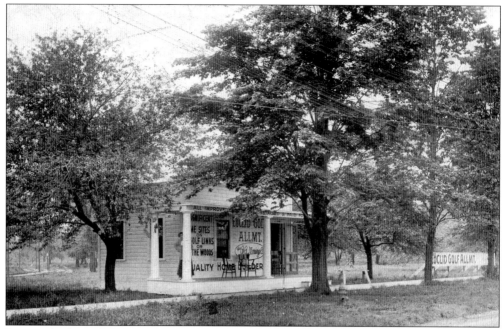

Deming had two different on-site allotment offices. The first, pictured here in this May 1913 photograph, was located at 2380 Coventry Road. It sat approximately on what is currently the front lawn of St. Paul's Church. Notice to the left of the photograph that Fairmount Boulevard has not yet been constructed on either side of the tracks. Notice also the long billboard fronting Coventry on the right hand side of the photograph. (Weston Schmitt.)

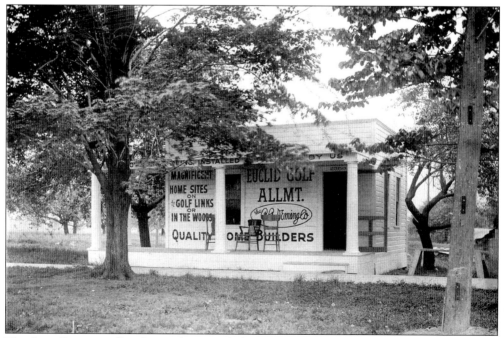

The first allotment office featured some splashy advertising. Home buyers had their choice of lots in the woods or in the open, on what had been the golf links. (Weston Schmitt.)

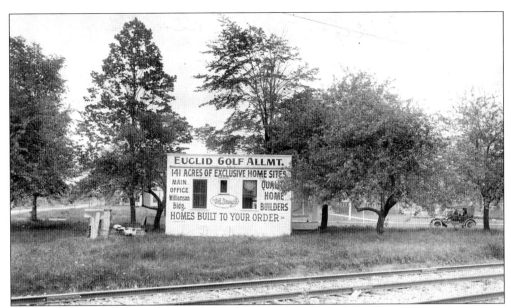

This is the rear of the Coventry Road office, with yet more advertising! The automobile is headed northbound on Coventry. The street seen to the left of the photograph is Coleridge Road where it meets Coventry. (Weston Schmitt.)

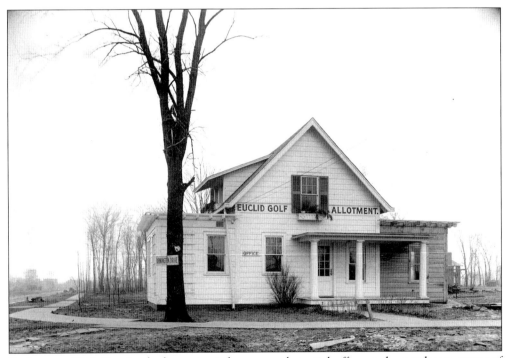

By January 1914, Deming had constructed a more substantial office at the northeast corner of Fairmount and Demington. This time he dispensed with garish advertising graphics and instead opted for window boxes and trellis work. Notice that he has already added on to the right side of the building! Take out your magnifying glass (we obviously have), look to the right of the allotment office, and you'll see the shell of 2270 Chatfield Drive as it is being constructed. (RSA.)

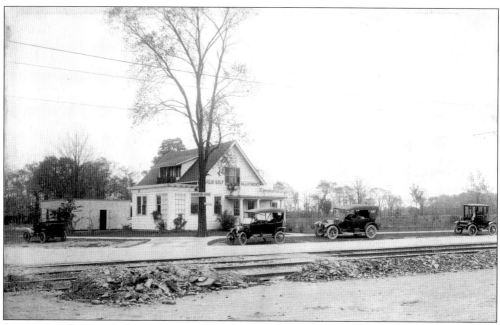

This is the allotment office at Demington and Fairmount in October 1914. Motor by, stop in, select house designs by Howell & Thomas, and choose a lot. Or, bring your own architect and builder. The automobiles pictured include two Ford Model Ts to the left and to the right, what appears to be a Cleveland-made Baker Electric. We've not identified the large touring car. Deming sold the 300-foot parcel on which the office stood in 1924 to builder William Cunningham. (Weston Schmitt.)

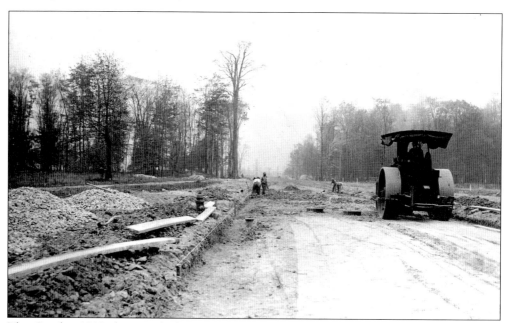

This October 1913 photograph shows a steam roller preparing Demington Drive for pavement. It is taken looking north from Fairmount Boulevard. Notice the sewer caps in the street, the fire hydrant, and the string lines demarcating the edge of the pavement. (RSA.)

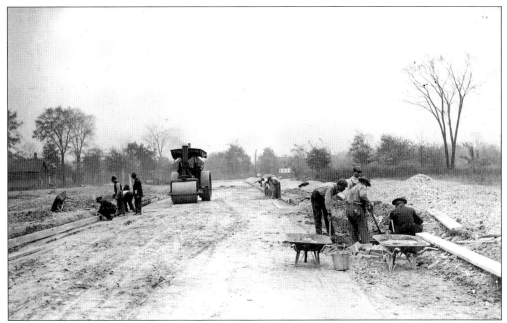

This photograph, also dated October 1913, again shows Demington Drive, this time from Nottinghill Lane looking north toward Cedar Road. While the shanty from previous photographs is gone, this shot reveals another modest dwelling fronting Cedar on the left. It seems out of place next to the neighboring mansions along Cedar. Note that the land to the right in the photograph is not a part of Euclid Golf. (RSA.)

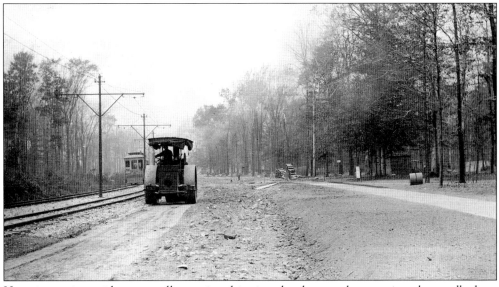

Here is our intrepid steam roller again, this time hard at work preparing the roadbed on Fairmount Boulevard just west of Demington Drive. Notice the trolley on its way eastward, and that the eastbound side of Fairmount has not yet been laid. The construction activity on the right side of the photograph relates to 2645 Fairmount Boulevard, the first house Deming built, which would have been well under way as of this October 1913 shot. (RSA.)

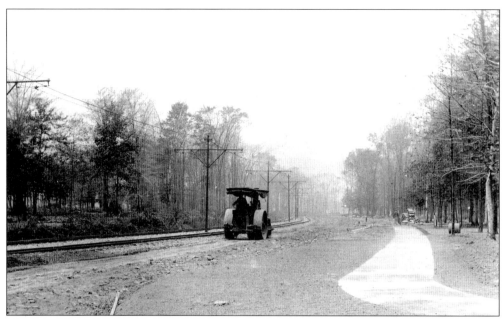

Our steam roller is shown here again in a photograph taken looking west from Demington Drive. Note that the sandstone sidewalks have already been laid as of October 1913. (RSA.)

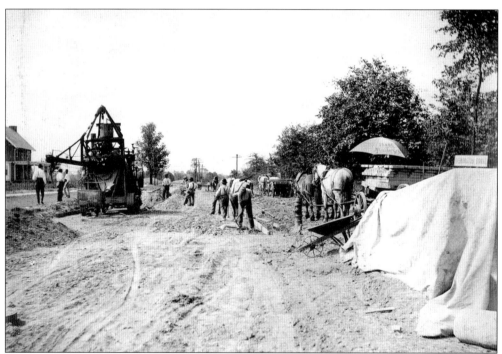

Street construction at the time involved the combination of man power, horse power, and steam power! This photograph, dated June 1914, shows the construction of Demington Drive and is taken looking south from Fairmount Boulevard. The house to the left is 2357 Demington Drive. This house is one of the first constructed by Deming and was completed prior to a road being in place! See the photograph of the house on the opposite page. (RSA.)

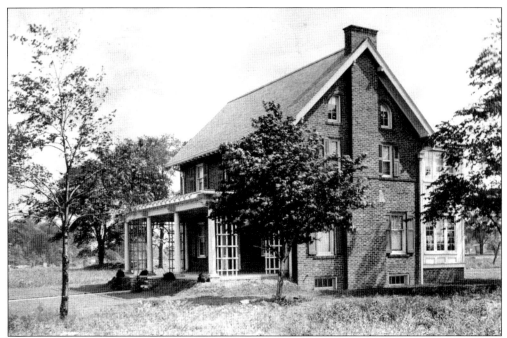

2357 Demington Drive, in a photograph taken *c.* 1915, was one of the first houses Deming built in early 1914 (the permit was pulled on December 20, 1913). Designed by Howell & Thomas, the original drawings show this house to be rare for Euclid Golf in several respects. First, it had a full length front porch, and second, it has since lost this lovely feature. We know of no other Euclid Golf houses that have lost a major design element. (RSA.)

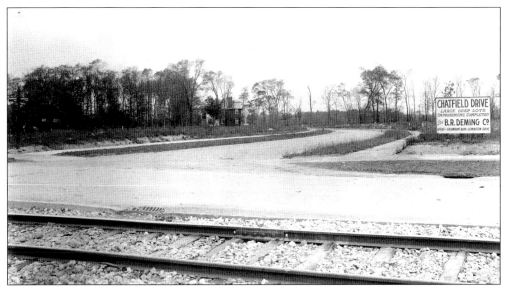

By April 1914, Chatfield Drive had its first house completed. 2270 Chatfield was designed by Howell & Thomas and was built by Deming. Each street sported an advertising sign such as this one, undoubtedly designed to attract the attention of riders on the trolley. Despite Deming making the claim that "improvements" were completed, the street is as yet unpaved! This photograph was taken looking north from Fairmount Boulevard. (RSA.)

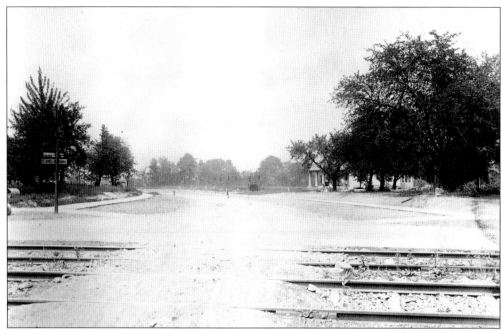

A careful look at this picture of North Saint James Parkway shows the original street signs Deming erected in Euclid Golf. They feature ornate poles with ironwork brackets from which the street signs are hung. The trees in this picture are the remains of the orchard that covered this end of Euclid Golf. The house behind the trees is 2325 North Saint James. This picture is taken looking north from Fairmount Boulevard and is dated August 1914. (RSA.)

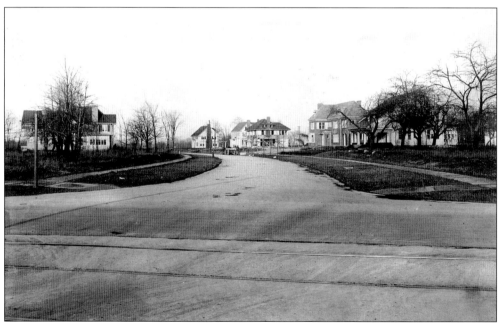

By December 1915, North Saint James Parkway had been built-up considerably. The horse and wagon in front of the house under construction reveals that even as late as 1915, machines had not yet completely taken over. (RSA.)

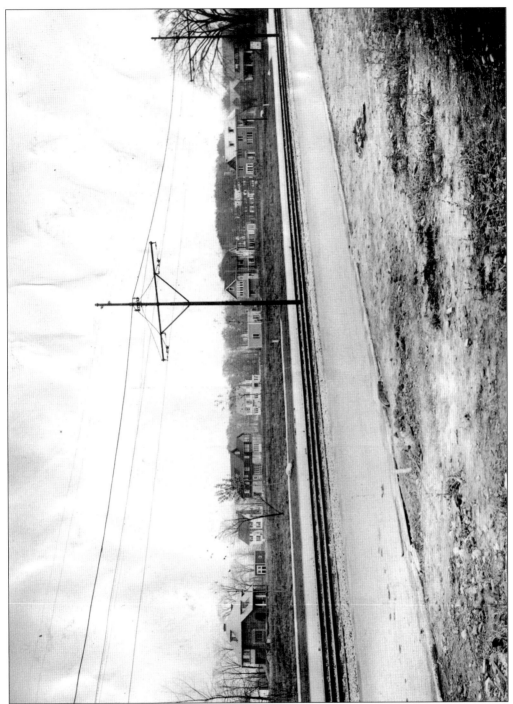

This rare panorama shot is dated November 1915 and looks northeast from Demington Drive and Fairmount Boulevard. The two houses on the left are on Chatfield Drive; the others are on North Saint James Parkway. Also visible are a few houses on Coventry Road that are not a part of Euclid Golf. The eastern portion of the Euclid Golf land was fairly open, but had never been laid out as a part of the golf links. (RSA.)

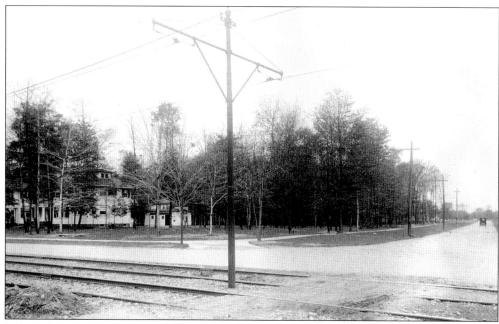

This is the northwest corner of Demington Drive and Fairmount Boulevard in a photograph dated October 1914. The house is 2645 Fairmount Boulevard, the first that Deming built, along with its motor house with quarters above. Note the construction debris at the temporary track crossing, as well as the automobile motoring northbound on Demington Drive. (RSA.)

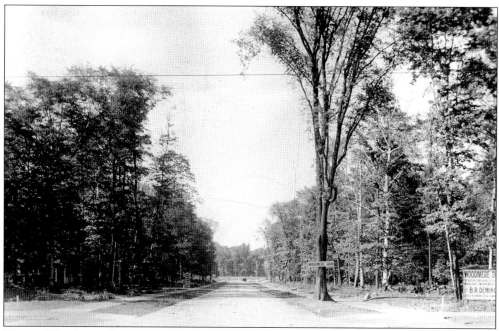

This is Woodmere Drive in a June 1915 photograph taken looking north from Fairmount Boulevard toward Nottinghill Lane. This section in the center of the Euclid Gold land was obviously heavily wooded. The house hiding in the trees on the left hand side of the photograph is 2280 Woodmere, one of the earliest houses Deming built. (RSA.)

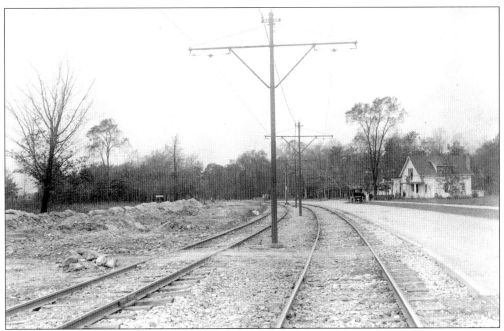

This October 1914 shot shows how unimproved the southern portion of Euclid Golf is compared to the section north of the trolley tracks. The photograph is taken looking west from Chatfield Drive and shows the allotment office at Demington and Fairmount, as well as 2645 Fairmount Boulevard, obscured by trees just beyond the allotment office. (RSA.)

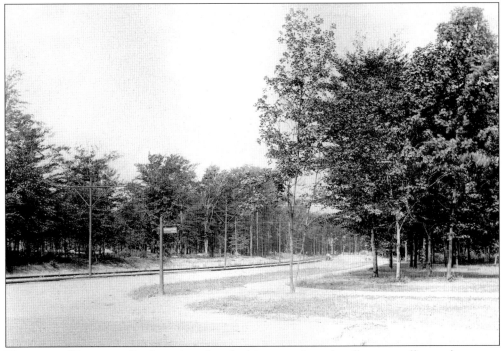

This view of Fairmount Boulevard is taken looking west from the allotment office at the corner of Demington Drive and Fairmount. The photograph is dated June 1914. (RSA.)

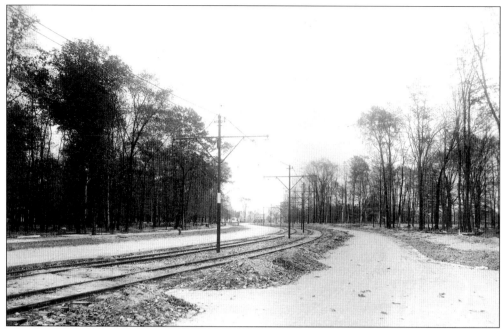

This view of Fairmount Boulevard is taken looking east from Roxboro Road. The light colored building in the distance is the allotment office at Demington and Fairmount. The photograph is dated April 1914. (RSA.)

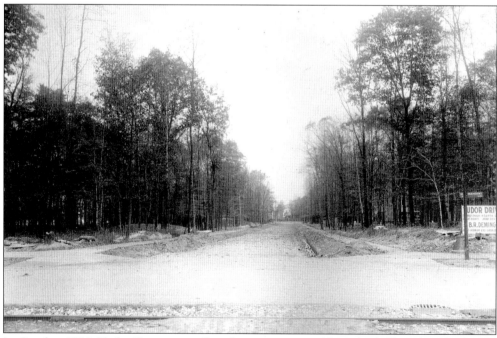

In October 1914, Tudor Drive was still under construction. Note the billboard at the foot of the street. The lone house on Tudor at this time, obscured by the trees on the right hand side of the photograph and still under construction as well, is 2275 Tudor. The photograph is taken looking north from Fairmount Boulevard toward Nottinghill Lane. (RSA.)

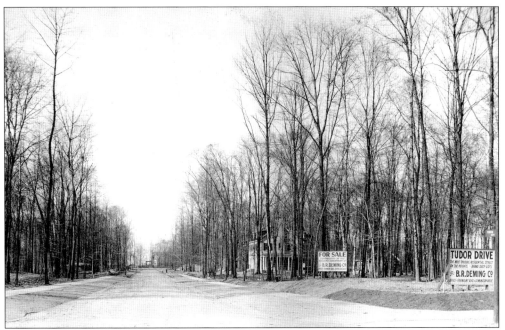

This is Tudor Drive again in a photograph dated February 1915. 2275 Tudor and its garage appear to be well on toward completion. The house in the distance at the end of the street fronts onto Cedar Road. (RSA.)

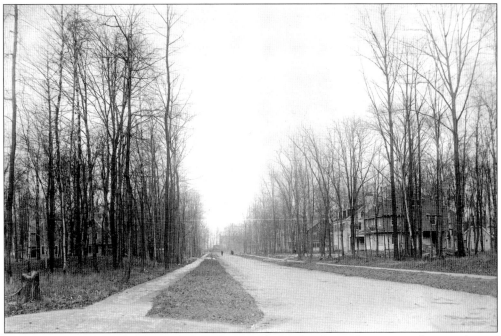

By December 1915, the date of this photograph, Tudor Drive has acquired a number of additional houses. On the left side of the street is 2270 Tudor. On the right side of the street, starting from the foreground are 2281, 2275, and 2257 Tudor. All are Howell & Thomas designs built by Barton Deming. (RSA.)

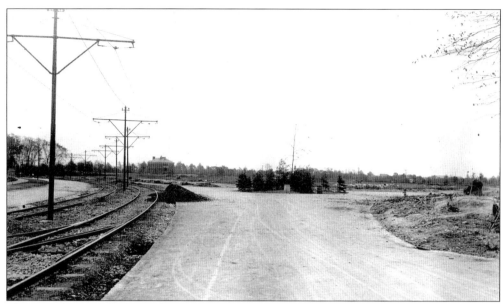

This rare photograph shows the southern-most section of Euclid Golf. Deming developed this section later, and consequently there are few early views of this land under construction. Taken at Fairmount Boulevard and Upper Drive the picture shows Ardleigh Drive branching off to the right and the small garden circle that exists today. Deming had already planted the circle as of this October 1914 photograph. Notice Roxboro School in the distance. (RSA.)

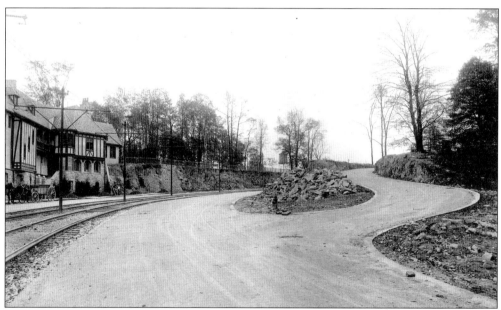

This October 1914 photograph shows Deming's house with horse and wagon in front of it and Upper Drive, a short access road that parallels Fairmount Boulevard. Anyone who enters the rear parking lot of the Fairmount Medical Arts Building drives across the entrance to Upper Drive as shown here. The upper portion of this drive services three Fairmount Boulevard houses. A careful examination of the center of the photograph reveals a conical water tower perched on the ridge. (RSA.)

# Four

# HOMES OF EUCLID GOLF

Following Garden City principles, Euclid Golf was designed to take advantage of the natural beauty of its environment. As Deming said in his very first Euclid Golf advertisement in *Cleveland Town Topics*: "The natural beauty of this property suggests and demands the upbuilding of a community of homes of refinement and character." The change in grade at the intersection of Fairmount Boulevard and Cedar Road forms a majestic entrance to the allotment. The gentle curving side streets make the most of natural vantage points and add a picturesque quality to the housing sites. A planted circle graces the intersection of Ardleigh Drive and Fairmount Boulevard. Homes are designed in a wide variety of eclectic American and European revival styles. Yet, they blend harmoniously with the landscape and with each other due to features such as high-quality, natural materials, uniform setbacks, and regulated investment levels. Garages and utility lines are behind the homes where they do not interfere with the garden-like aesthetic. Deming worked to preserve many of the mature trees that existed during the property's golf course days. Additional street trees were planted to create a green canopy.

Seven deed restrictions, in force until May 1, 1950, spelled out setback requirements, minimum construction costs, and prohibited uses. Houses were to be "exclusively for private dwelling house purposes." Minimum investment levels and setback requirements varied according to where the house was built within the allotment. Although the architectural style was not specified, the B.R. Deming Company approved all plans and specifications for each house. Deming hired architects Howell & Thomas to design a variety of housing styles to fit the varied lots and sizes. These model homes set high standards and reduced the risk of appearing arbitrary in enforcing the restrictions.

Setbacks and minimum investment levels were specified for fences, garages, and outbuildings. Separate "water-closets" were prohibited, as were various "undesirable uses," such as public entertainment houses, apartment houses, boarding-houses, hotels, taverns, dance halls, or other resorts. The manufacture or sale of "spirituous, vinous, or fermented liquors" was strictly prohibited, and the use of advertising signs and devices that would endanger or disturb the neighbors were severely restricted. A requirement that the landscaping be maintained in accordance with the standards set by the B.R. Deming Company appears to have been added later.

In addition to Howell & Thomas, architects of local and national distinction such as Best & Hoefler, Bohnard & Parsson, Harold Burdick, George H. Burrows, Copper & Dunn, Harold O. Fullerton, Charles R. Greco, Reynold H. Hinsdale, Arthur E. Keller, Joseph M. Miller, Maxwell Norcross, Meade & Hamilton, Harry Porter, Philip E. Robinson, Charles Schneider, and Walker & Weeks designed homes in Euclid Golf. Colonial Revival and Tudor Revival are the most dominant styles. However, examples of French Renaissance, Italian Renaissance, Shingle, Prairie, and Arts and Crafts also exist. Many homes are truly eclectic in that they combine elements of two or more styles. The picturesque and romantic eclecticism of the homes probably gave early twentieth century Clevelanders a sense of safety and security in a rapidly industrializing and changing society.

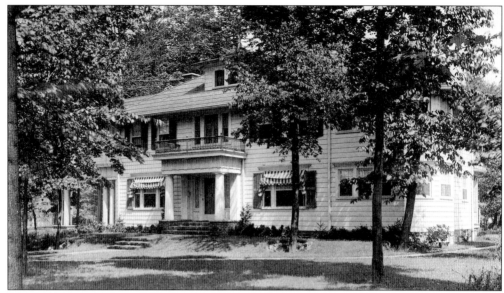

On June 20, 1913, Deming took out a permit to build his first Euclid Golf house at 2645 Fairmount Boulevard. Designed by architect P.E. Robinson, the *Cleveland Leader* proclaimed, "an attractive colonial type of house inaugurates the home building at (the) Euclid Golf Allotment." The dormer is absent in the original architectural rendering. The ashes of first owners J.H. and Emma Smith are reputedly buried in the back yard. Smith was a lawyer with the firm Smith & Weber. (RSA.)

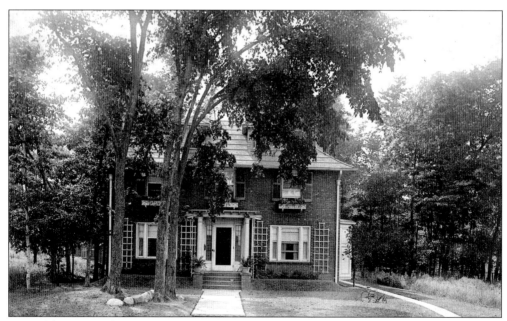

One of the very earliest houses Deming built was 2270 Chatfield Drive. Its original owner was Clyde S. Pelton, a department manager at Perfection Spring Company. Designed by Howell & Thomas and combining Prairie and Craftsman influences, it was completed in early 1914. An impressive garage with quarters above was added in 1919. Notice the window boxes and trellises, as well as the child's tricycle on the front lawn. The photograph is dated August 1916. (RSA.)

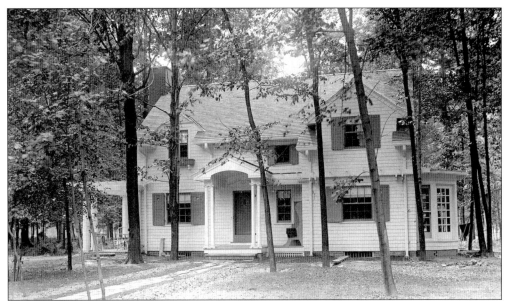

Another early house is 2280 Woodmere, built by Deming, who took out a permit for it on February 11, 1914. The photograph is dated July 1914. With the exception of 2645 Fairmount, the first few houses Deming constructed were more modest than the grand revival style houses that would come later. One of Euclid Golf's distinguishing characteristics is the diversity of house styles and sizes, appealing to a wider variety of tastes and pocketbooks. The architect of this house is unknown. (RSA.)

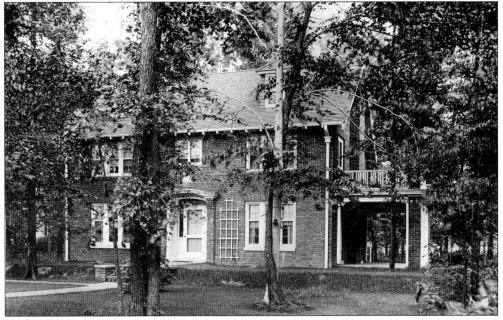

2263 Demington Drive is one of the earliest houses Deming constructed. Built in 1914, this brick colonial features three-part windows, a side porch, two dormers, and exposed rafters. A stone medallion is inset into the brick above the graceful entryway. Howell & Thomas are the architects. This photograph is dated July 1915. (RSA.)

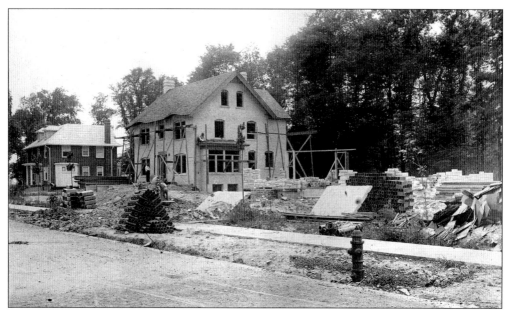

This August 1914 photograph documents houses on Chatfield Drive at various stages of completion. At left is 2270 Chatfield. Next is 2260 Chatfield, designed by architect Otto Staff, mid-way through construction. In the foreground is 2252 Chatfield in its very earliest stages of construction. Notice the piles of drain tile, the workmen, and to the right, a pile of pre-stained wood shakes. Chatfield Drive has yet to be paved. (RSA.)

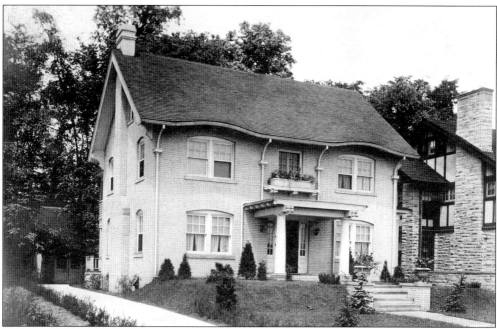

This July 1916 photograph shows 2260 Chatfield in its completed state. Its original owner, Otto I. Leisy, was the secretary-treasurer of the Leisy-Patton Company, toolmakers. In 1915, Leisy added the garage just visible in the picture—an impressive building in its own right complete with a turntable on which to turn one's car around to make a quick exit! (RSA.)

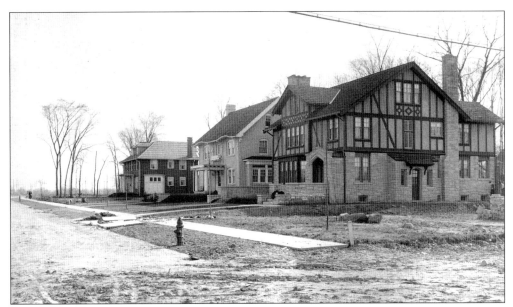

By this March 1915 photograph, the three Chatfield houses shown on the opposite page have been completed. On the right is 2252 Chatfield, built by Deming for Frederick D. Kellogg. Howell & Thomas designed a Tudor inspired house that makes extensive use of random ashlar and cut stone, appropriate given that Kellogg was president of Ohio Cut Stone Company. Note the newly laid sandstone sidewalks, largely intact today. (RSA.)

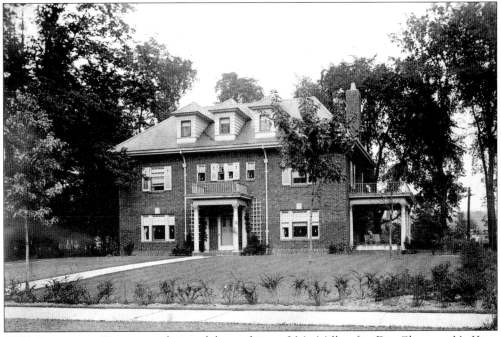

2287 Demington Drive was designed by architect J.M. Miller for Dr. Clarence V. Kerr, president of the Cleveland Osteopathic Clinic. This house was featured in the June 1916 edition of *The Ohio Architect, Engineer and Builder*, along with plans for a garden design, not realized, by landscape architect Louis Brandt. This photograph is dated August 1916. (RSA.)

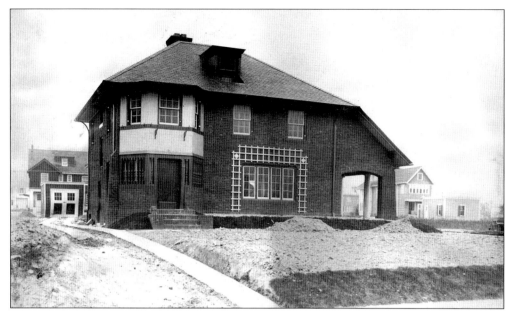

Architects Bohnard & Parsson designed this house at 2289 Chatfield Drive for Louis Englander in 1915. Notice the subtle buttress to the left of the entrance bay, as well as the matching form to the right of the porch opening. Bohnard & Parsson had diverse ability, but were especially accomplished designers of English Arts and Crafts inspired homes, a hint of which can be seen in this house. The photograph is dated October 1915. (RSA.)

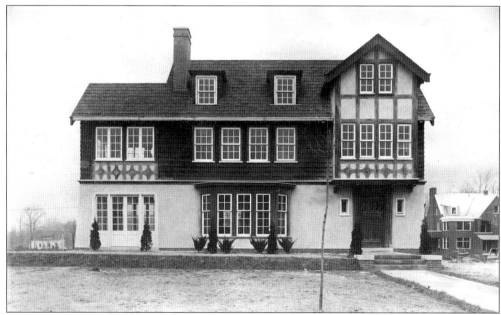

This Tudor-inspired house at 2290 North Saint James Parkway was designed by Howell & Thomas and built by Deming in 1915. It has just been completed in this November 1915 photograph. The design for this house combines stucco, clapboards, half timbering, and a wood roof. The house visible to the right is the rear of 2277 Chatfield, under construction. The building in the distance to the left is Deming's allotment office at Fairmount and Demington. (RSA.)

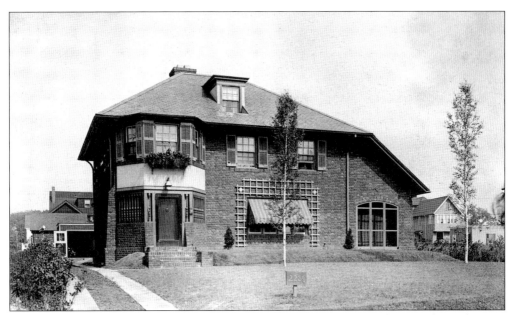

Nearly a year later, 2289 Chatfield has been landscaped and trimmed out with its shutters, window box, and awning. The owner of the house, Louis Englander, would unfortunately not enjoy his house much longer as he would die in 1920 at the young age of 37. Englander was an attorney with the firm Englander & Bowden. The simple one-stall garage in the rear would be replaced later with the far more substantial brick building that exists today. (RSA.)

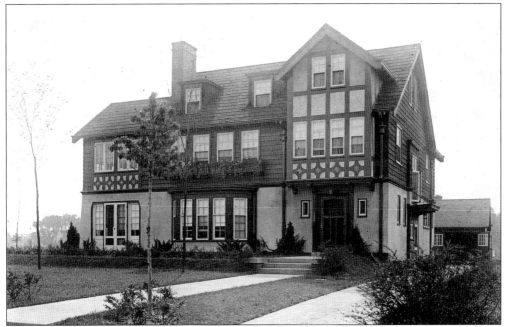

It is summer, and 2290 North Saint James has been landscaped. Finishing touches include the long window box, as well as downspouts. The paint scheme has been subtly altered, with dark paint having been applied to the small windows flanking the front door, as well as to the trim surrounding the sun porch on the left. (RSA.)

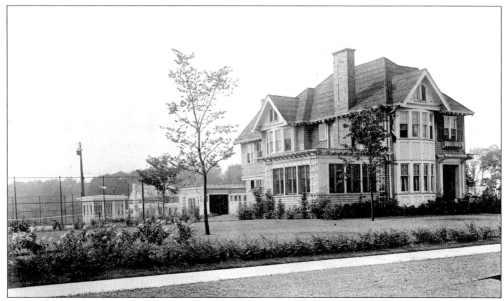

In early 1914, Deming built this house at 2312 North Saint James for George H. and Cora Miller. Howell & Thomas designed an eclectic shingled house with Craftsman details and a wood roof. The original drawings for this house include a garden design incorporating a tennis court, seen to the left in the photograph. Later, this house would receive a massive three-storey addition in place of the sun room. The photograph is dated August 1916. (RSA.)

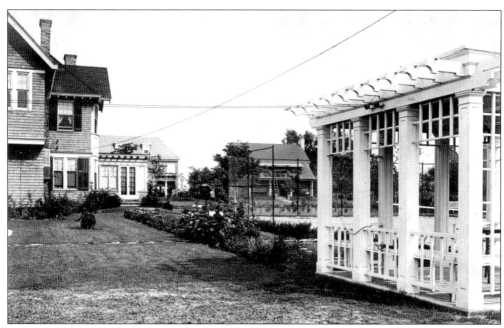

This rear view of 2312 North Saint James shows the Howell & Thomas designed garden pergola that would have made a fine spot to sit and watch a tennis match. Owner George H. Miller originally owned a hardware store, but later invested in and became the secretary-treasurer of the Musterole Company, the manufacturer of the famous mustard ointment of the same name used for chest congestion and muscle aches. (RSA.)

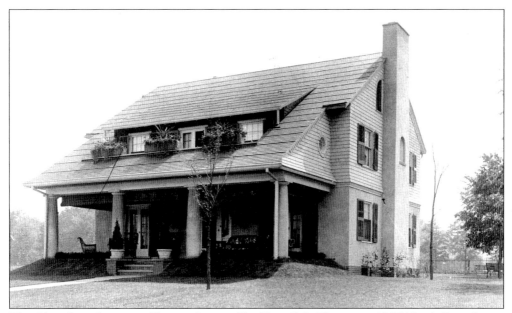

This Shingle-style inspired house, designed by Howell & Thomas at 2325 North Saint James Parkway, was the only Euclid Golf home to appear in the 1917 publication of *Beautiful Homes of Cleveland*. Built by Deming in 1914, it features a shingled second storey over stucco and a wood roof. Robust stucco-clad Doric columns support its full-length front porch. In this August 1915 photograph, owner W.B. Alexander has outfitted the porch with wicker furniture and grass blinds. (RSA.)

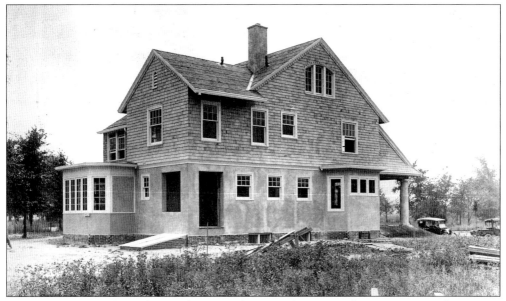

William Brownlie Alexander was the original owner of 2325 North Saint James Parkway, seen here from the rear in this June 1914 photograph. Alexander was a superintendent with the National Screw and Tack Company. Alexander's father, W.D.B. Alexander, was the president of the company. The debris visible in this photograph is appropriate given that the house is still under construction. (RSA.)

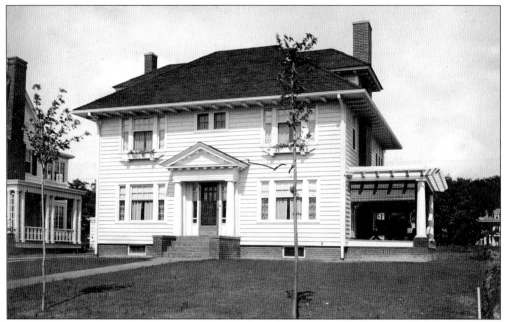

2295 North Saint James was constructed in 1915 by builder F.C. Smith, who is also listed as its architect. This house is best described as "eclectic," with clapboard siding, a hipped roof with deep eves and chunky modillions, an entrance featuring classical pediment and columns, a trellised side porch, and window boxes carrying forward the trellis theme. The original owner was Edward A. France, a manager with the Jones & Laughlin Steel Corporation. This photograph is dated July 1916. (RSA.)

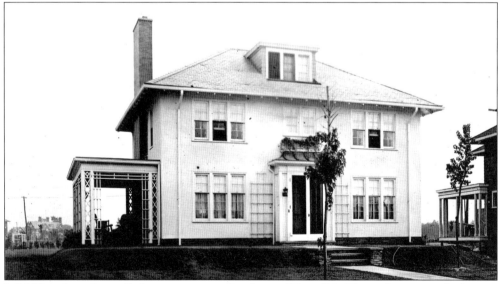

2696 West Saint James Parkway is an example of one of Howell & Thomas' more simple designs. Built by Deming in 1915, it features clean stucco walls and identical tripartite windows, which are a backdrop for details such as the wall trellises, window box, and elegant entrance portico with curved, standing-seam roof. Original owner Brewster Kinney was vice president of Kinney & Levan, china and crockery wholesalers. The photograph is dated August 1916. (RSA.)

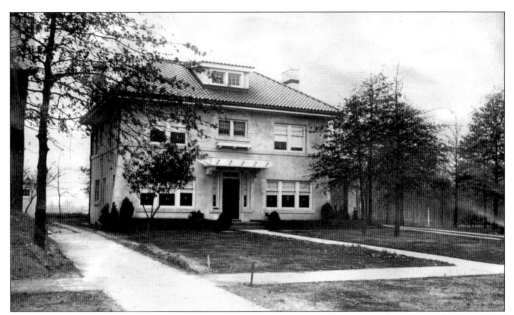

Architect Joseph M. Miller's design for 2364 Demington Drive typifies the eclecticism of early twentieth century homes. While the stucco walls and tile roof suggest Italian influences, the strong horizontality formed by the first storey windows and beltline are Prairie. The flared corners of the first storey further the Prairie effect by pulling the house into the landscape. Built in 1915 for Albion M. Tousley, the house was pictured in the June 1916 *Ohio Architect, Engineer and Builder*. (RSA.)

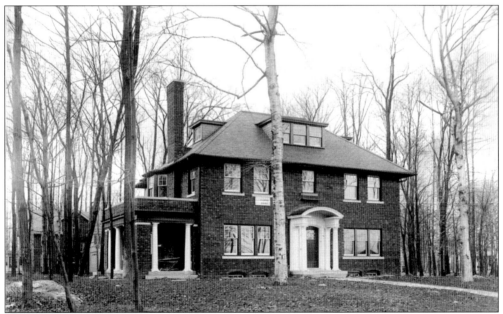

Architects Steffens and Steffens designed this house at 2256 Woodmere Drive. John F. Steffens also designed the Heights Medical Arts Building on Fairmount Boulevard. This photograph, dated December 1915, was taken shortly after builder W.W. Jepson completed the house. Jepson's sign can be seen hanging from a second-storey window. (RSA.)

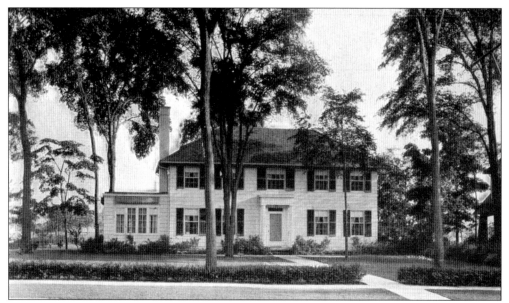

In 1918, Deming built this house for widow Ida A. Scofield. Her late husband William C. Scofield founded Lake Erie Iron Company. Howell & Thomas designed 2650 Fairmount Boulevard in a simple Colonial style, with whitewashed shingle siding, shutters, and a classical entryway. The hipped roof shows Craftsman influence with exposed rafters. The rear of the house has irregular massing and a trellised entryway giving it a cottage-like feel. This image is taken from Deming's later brochure published c.1921. (Weston Schmitt.)

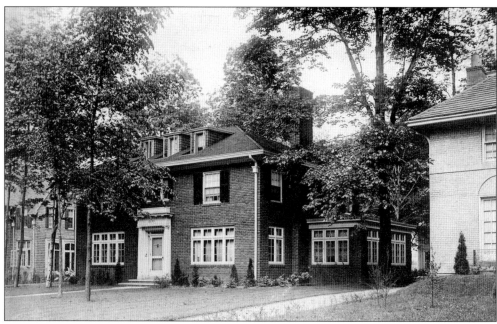

2235 Tudor Drive was built in 1916 by Deming and was originally owned by Richard C. Bourne, a salesman. Howell & Thomas' simple, brick-Colonial design featuring a hipped roof, deep eves, and large dormers was a common residential style at the time. This photograph is dated June 1917. (RSA.)

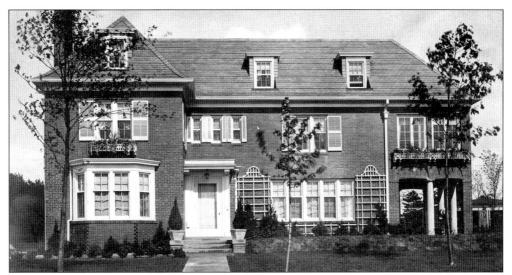

Deming built 2319 North Saint James Parkway in 1915 for Joseph and Mary Burton. Burton was general manager of Burton Explosives division of American Cyanamid and Chemical Corporation. This Howell & Thomas design is French in flavor owing to its steeply pitched hipped roof with flared eves. Other features include patterned brick arches over the windows on the main block, as well as over the side porch colonnade. Note the trellises and window boxes in this June 1916 photograph. (RSA.)

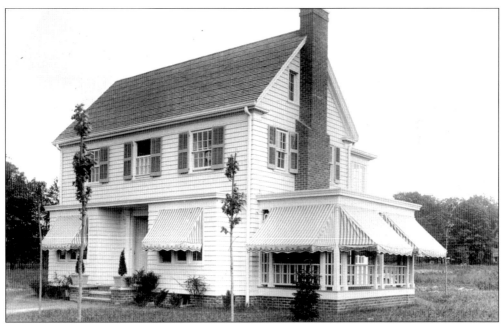

This simple Colonial at 2289 North Saint James Parkway was designed by Howell & Thomas and built by Deming in 1915. White clapboards, shutters, and eight-over-eight window sashes complete the Colonial look. The flat roofs on the unusual box bays extend to form a covered entryway. Early owner Sheldon K. Towson was vice president and assistant general manager of the Elwell-Parker Electric Company, manufacturers of electric lift trucks. Towson's father, Morris, was president. This photograph is dated August 1915. (RSA.)

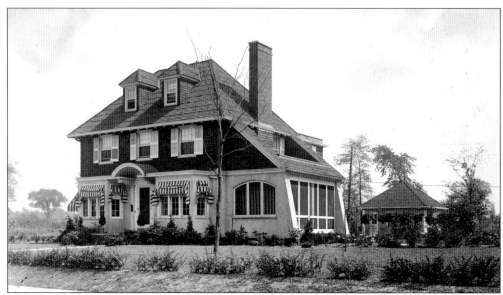

Howell & Thomas' design for 2235 Woodmere Drive features flat-topped bays and an integral side sun porch. The shingle over stucco house is larger than it appears, with a substantial rear wing not visible in the photograph. Deming built this house in 1915 and included a stucco garage. The photograph was taken *c.* 1916. (RSA.)

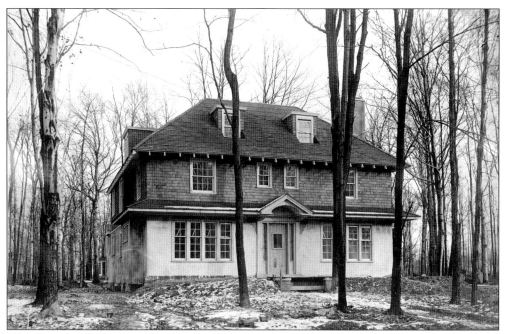

This Shingle style house at 2281 Tudor Drive was designed by Howell & Thomas and built by Deming in 1915. It features a stucco lower storey and wood-clad second storey, separated by a pent roof and hooded entry. The exposed rafter tails reveal Craftsman influence. The house is still under construction in this December 1915 photograph. Notice the temporary front door. The original owner was Lewis E. Dunham, who worked in the ore sales department of the M.A. Hanna Corporation. (RSA.)

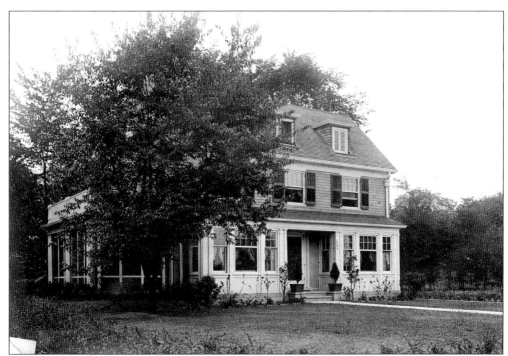

Deming completed this quaint Colonial at 2234 Woodmere Drive in 1916. The Howell & Thomas design incorporates large bays topped by a shed roof that serves as a covered entryway. The bays are completely cased and paneled, and with the addition of pilaster detailing, they stand in contrast to the simple wood shingles covering the second storey. The original owner of this house was Alfred B. Emery, vice president of Cleveland Material Company. The photograph is dated August 1916. (RSA.)

The Dutch Colonial style was popular at the time, but remains fairly rare in Euclid Golf. This house, located at 2276 North Saint James Parkway, is a simple three-ranked design with clapboard lower storey and shingled second storey. It was designed by Howell & Thomas and built by Deming in 1916. The photograph is dated June 1917. (RSA.)

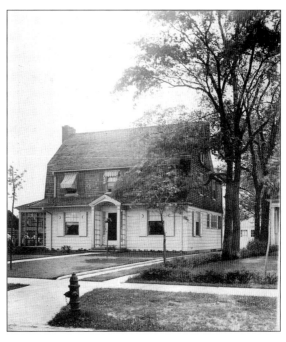

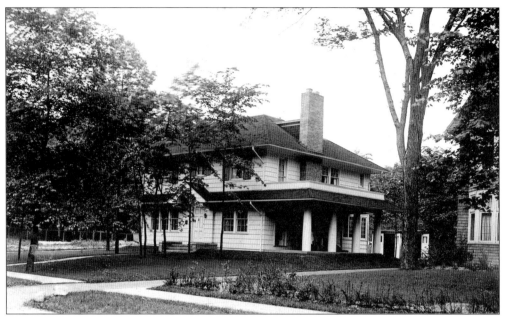

Attorney Leroy B. Davenport was the original owner of 2221 Tudor Drive. Its simple Colonial design incorporates a pent roof that encircles the side porch. The house was designed in 1916 by the architectural firm Steffens and Steffens. John F. Steffens was the architect of the Heights Medical Arts Building at the foot of Fairmount Boulevard. (RSA.)

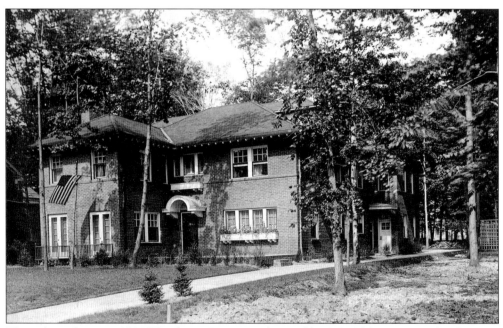

This eclectic house at 2281 Woodmere Drive was designed by R.S. Silsbee in 1916 for physician Harry G. Sloan. It is a mixture of design elements, ranging from formal French doors with decorative iron railings on the lower level, to informal Craftsman-inspired exposed rafter tails at the top. The prominently displayed American flag is likely reflective of President Wilson declaring war on Germany just a few months prior to this photograph being taken in June 1917. (RSA.)

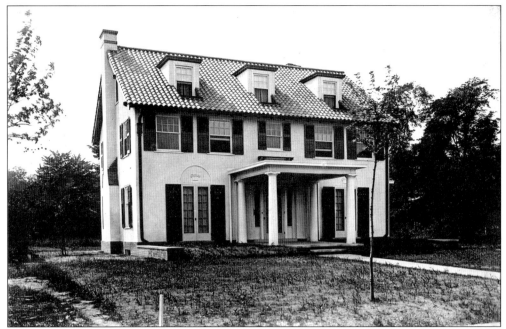

Howell & Thomas designed this eclectic stucco-clad house at 2288 Chatfield Drive. The tiled roof, punctuated by flat-topped dormers, features open eves with exposed rafters and false beams on the gable ends. Four Doric columns, with triglyphs appropriately aligned over each, support a large porch. The foundation walls extend out into the landscape—a common Howell & Thomas touch. Deming completed the house in 1916 for Frank J. Venning, the president of Union Salt Company. (RSA.)

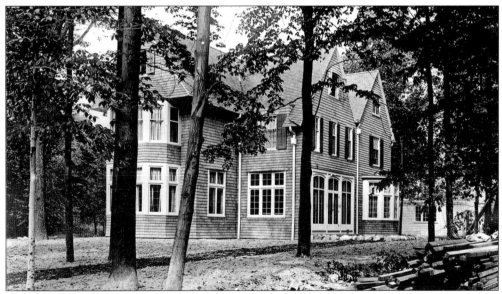

This narrow, but deep, Shingle style house is located at 2227 Tudor Drive. A prominent two-storey bay dominates the facade facing the street, while dramatic parallel gables dominate the sides. The entryway is on the side opposite the camera in this picture dated August 1916. Howell & Thomas are the architects. Deming completed the house in 1916 for widow Frances C. Mason. (RSA.)

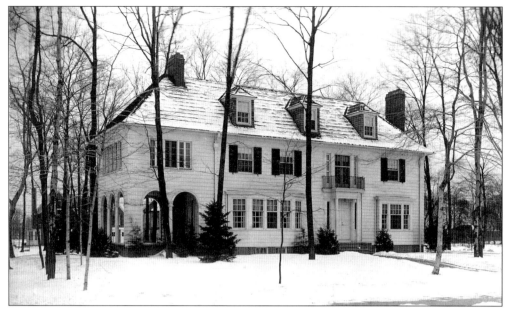

This large Colonial at 2224 Tudor Drive sits on a double lot. Designed by Howell & Thomas, the original owner was Randolph G. Pack. In the May 1921 article about Euclid Golf in *The Architectural Forum*, the Pack house is described as having seven different types of openings in its façade and being "a most interesting expression of an asymmetric plan." Deming built the house in 1917. The photograph is dated January 1918. (RSA.)

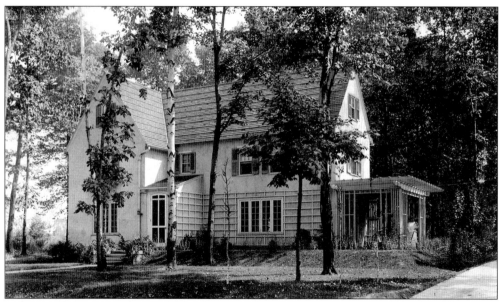

2257 Woodmere Drive borrows from the English Arts and Crafts movement. Its clean, simple form, dominant front-facing gable, smooth stucco walls, and steeply pitched roof create a backdrop for vines to grow on the extensive trellis. The side porch is actually a lacy garden pergola. Notice the trademark Howell & Thomas shed roof entryway. Deming completed the house in 1915 for Frances R. Marvin, a lawyer with the firm Marvin & Marvin. This photograph was taken *c.* 1916. (RSA.)

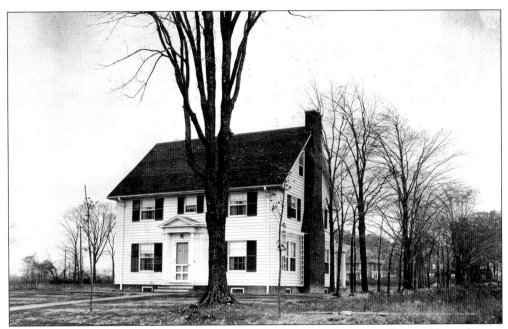

This modest Colonial located at 2271 North Saint James Parkway was designed by architects Dercum & Beer. It was built in 1915 for Walter S. Pope, an instructor at Western Reserve University. The houses visible in the distance are on Coventry Road and are not a part of Euclid Golf. This photograph is dated November 1915. (RSA.)

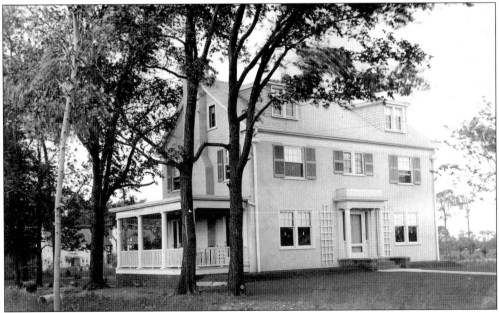

2270 North Saint James Parkway is another example of a somewhat more modest Euclid Golf house. It is a clean, stucco-clad Colonial with restrained detailing, large dormers, and a typical side porch. Built by Deming in 1915, the architect is unknown, though we would suspect it to be a Howell & Thomas design. The first owner was Walter B. Vaughn, who was employed in commercial traveling. The photograph is dated July 1915. (RSA.)

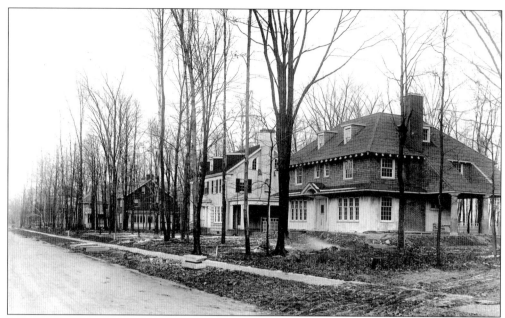

This Tudor Drive scene provides a glimpse of the level of development Deming had achieved as of this December 1915 photograph. Most of the first houses built were on streets north of Fairmount, such as this block of Tudor. Starting from the foreground, the houses pictured are 2281, 2275, 2257, and 2243. (RSA.)

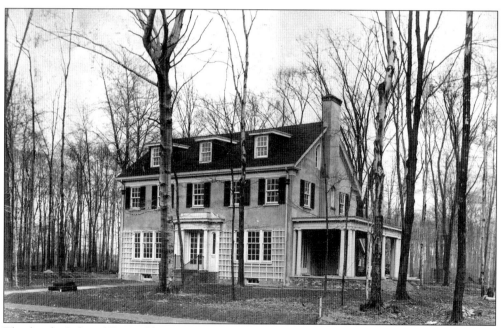

This lovely Colonial Revival house at 2275 Tudor Drive was designed by Howell & Thomas and completed by Deming in early 1915. The stucco is a fine backdrop for extensive details, particularly the rich entryway complete with columns, triglyphs, scrolls, and round-topped sidelights. Note the arched window punctuating the chimney. The original owner was Edward P. Carter, a professor at Western Reserve University. The photograph is dated February 1915. (RSA.)

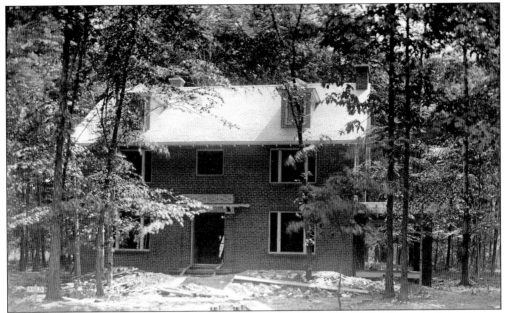

This July 1915 photograph documents 2257 Tudor Drive's construction. A Howell & Thomas design, it features Craftsman detailing such as open eaves with exposed rafter tails and a trellised entrance with planter box. Note the wall trellis lying on the sill of the lower left hand window, as well as the "sold" sign in the lower left corner of the photograph. Before its completion, the house would be altered. See the next photograph. (RSA.)

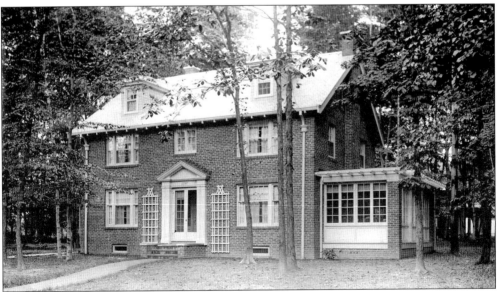

Here is 2257 Tudor Drive again, this time in September 1915. The completed house no longer has a Craftsman-inspired entry, but a traditional entrance with pediment and pilasters. Its other Craftsman details remain. The original drawings for this house feature the Craftsman entrance detail. The construction site change reflects either the taste of the new owner, Charles J. Estep, a judge in the court of common pleas, or Deming's shift from American forms to more European and classical forms. (RSA.)

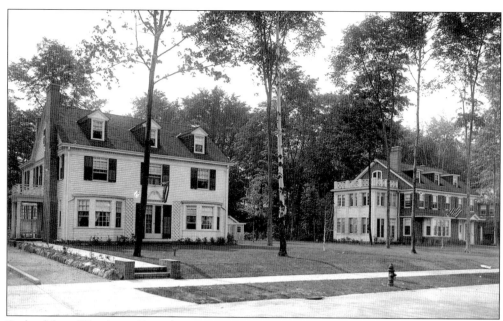

Both of these Woodmere Drive homes are Howell & Thomas designs built by Deming in 1916. On the left is 2272, owned by John C. McNutt, and on the right is 2268, owned by Lucia M. Curtiss. Although 2272 appears to be a classic Colonial design, it is actually a side-entry house with French doors in place of the centered entry. 2268 is an asymmetric Colonial Revival design with large bay, pent roof, and shingle cladding. (RSA.)

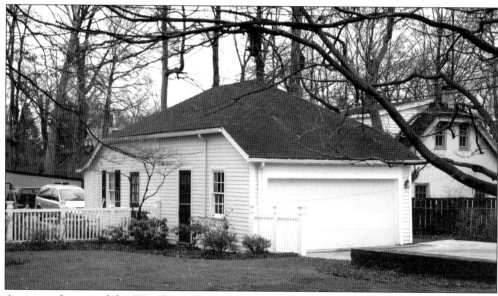

A unique feature of the Woodmere Drive homes shown above is that they share a garage, as seen in this modern photograph. The drive for 2272 is on the left and that of 2268 is on the right. The drives meet on opposite sides of the common garage structure, which creates a large green space between the houses. Mrs. Curtiss' daughter Anna was John McNutt's wife, hence the cooperation! McNutt was of the McNutt-McCall Company, a real estate and insurance concern. (Author Photo Collection.)

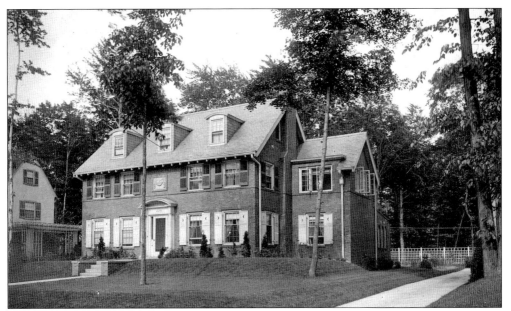

Deming built this Colonial Revival at 2265 Woodmere Drive in 1915. Architects Howell & Thomas' design incorporates an arched pediment over the front door, matching arched topped dormers and a decorative stone wall medallion featuring a swag motif. The shutters on the first storey windows are paneled; those on the second are louvered for ventilation. The open eves with exposed rafters lend an eclectic feel to the overall design. The photograph is dated June 1917. (RSA.)

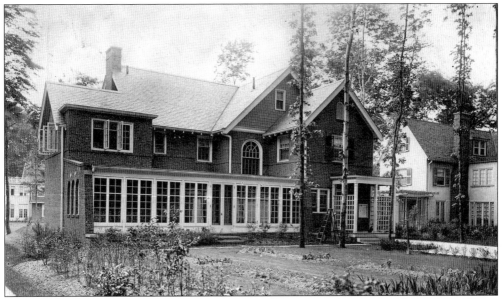

This photograph is a rare rear view of a Euclid Golf house, in this case 2265 Woodmere Drive again. Howell & Thomas designed a dramatic sun porch with extensive glazing and a row of arched windows in the end wall. A grand arched window looks out over the newly landscaped yard from the stair landing. The original owner of the house was William E. Curtiss, secretary-treasurer of the Cleveland Dental Manufacturing Company. This photograph is also dated June 1917. (RSA.)

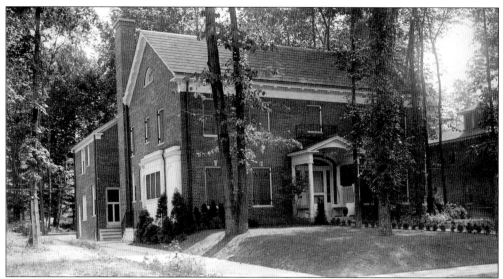

In 1915, Frank B. Meade of Meade & Hamilton designed this Colonial Revival house at 2275 Woodmere Drive for Clemens W. Lundoff, who was president of the Lundoff-Bicknell Company. Later, Warren Bicknell, chairman of the company, would have Meade & Hamilton design a grand mansion on Chestnut Hills Drive in nearby Ambler Heights. Lundoff-Bicknell were prolific commercial builders, including the Cleveland Public Library and the Higbee Department Store at the Terminal Tower complex. This photograph was taken *c.* 1916. (RSA.)

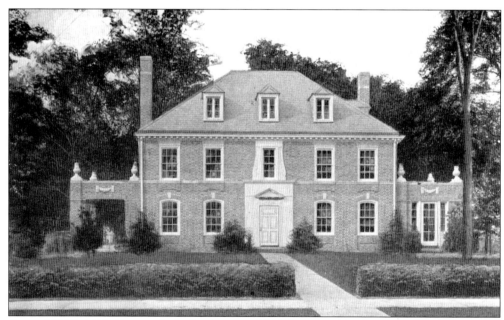

Around 1919–1920, Deming built this house at 2310 Coventry Road on speculation. Designed by Howell & Thomas, it is the archetypal Georgian Revival style featuring symmetrical façade with matching wings, hipped roof, and details such as dentil moldings, swags, and urns. This photograph, used in Deming's later brochure, was heavily re-touched to mask the fact that the house was as yet incomplete. A close look reveals that an artist added the door, windows, dormer pediments, and the landscaping! (Weston Schmitt.)

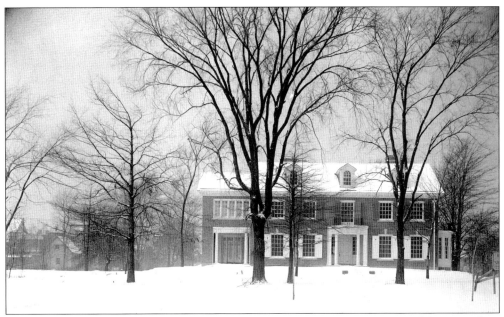

Another Deming-built spec house was 2520 Fairmount Boulevard. Designed by Howell & Thomas and erected in 1917, it features classic Colonial Revival details such as keystones, pedimented dormers with arched windows, and cornice with modillions and dentils. Notice the for sale sign on the right side. This photograph is dated January 1918. A March 1918 *Town Topics* advertisement invites a buyer to select the interior fixtures to "give the place the stamp of their individuality." (RSA.)

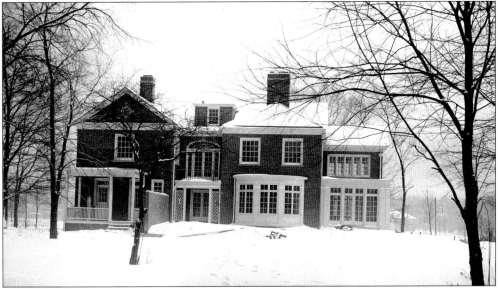

This photograph, also dated January 1918, shows the rear of 2520 Fairmount, revealing more details such as the elliptical fanlight over the French doors that lead to a small balcony, as well as the small round window with keystones that punctuates the main gable on the left. The home's first owner was Harry H. Hammond, treasurer of the McMyler Interstate Company, manufacturers of coal handling equipment and cranes, and a partner in the law firm White and Hammond. (RSA.)

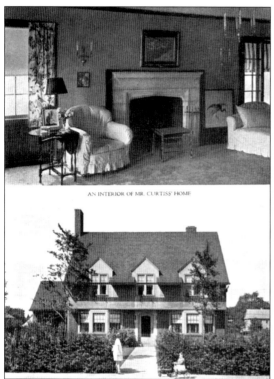

AN INTERIOR OF MR. CURTISS' HOME

This lovely English Cottage style house at 2322 Delamere Drive was designed by Howell & Thomas and built by Deming in 1917. The first owner was Henry S. Curtiss, a partner in the investment firm of Curtiss, House & Company. Deming used Curtiss' house to illustrate his later brochure and included this view of the living room with its comfortable, slip-covered furniture. (Weston Schmitt.)

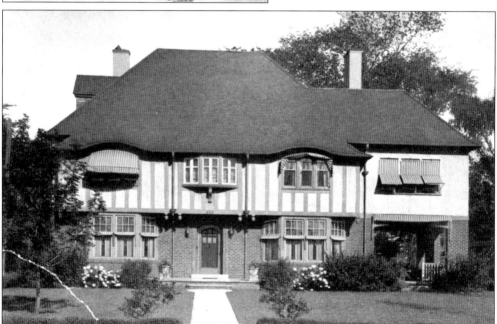

Howell & Thomas designed this English house for Mrs. Frances Allen at 2215 Delamere Drive. It was built by Deming in 1917. The house features a brick first storey with prominent bays. The overhanging second storey is half-timbered and features an oriel window. The hipped roof with its eyebrows over the windows seems to sit low on the house, completing the informal, English country look. The house was featured in Deming's later brochure. (Weston Schmitt.)

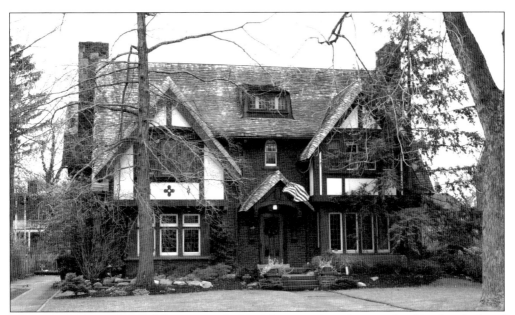

Harlen E. Shimmin designed this spectacular English-inspired residence with a false thatched roof at 2338 Ardleigh Drive. The roof, shown in this modern photograph, is covered in hand-formed wood shingles. Shimmin was a prolific architect whose houses can be found throughout Cleveland Heights, including others in Euclid Golf. The house was built in 1923. (Author photograph.)

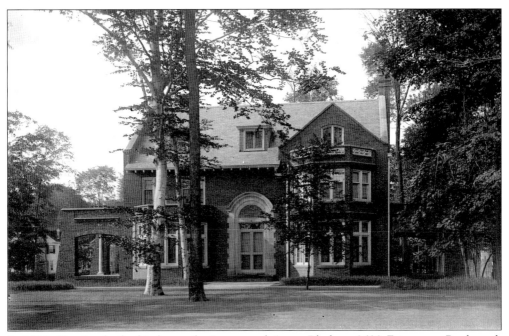

In 1916, Deming built this house for Lester and Anna Blyth at 2639 Fairmount Boulevard. Blyth was a partner in the Ernst & Ernst accounting firm. Howell & Thomas designed this brick, English-inspired house featuring prominent one and two storey bays, parapeted gables, and a dramatic entryway with a blind arch in cut stone. The house is bracketed by open porches. This photograph is dated June 1917. (RSA.)

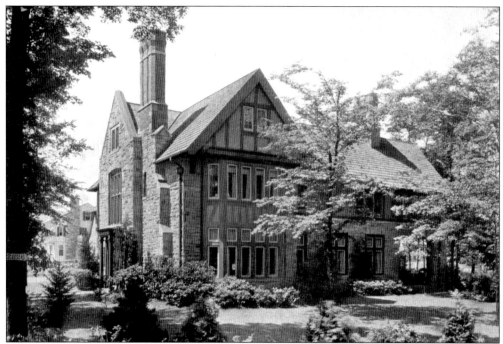

Attorney Fred Nichols was the first owner of 2626 Fairmount Boulevard. Built in 1916 by Deming, this accomplished Howell & Thomas design incorporates traditional Tudor materials such as stone, stucco, and half-timber. In a May 1921 *Architectural Forum* article about Euclid Golf, the author laments that the "restraining hand of economy has played its part and forbidden the necessary carving on the verge boards of the gable." Restraint, indeed! (Weston Schmitt.)

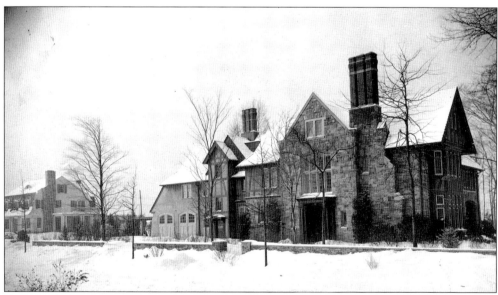

Here is 2626 Fairmount again, this time pictured in a winter scene dated January 1918. The aforementioned *Architectural Forum* article states: "The stonework of the Nichols residence is excellent, warm in color and of fine texture. It is all local material, having been taken from the excavation of a sewer in an adjoining street." (RSA.)

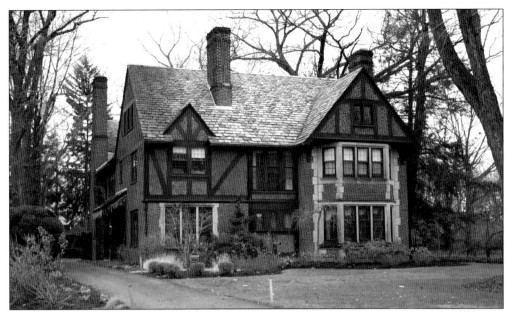

The prominent firm of Meade & Hamilton designed this lovely English inspired house at 2240 Delamere Drive. Note that the roof slates get progressively smaller toward the top, giving the illusion that the roof is taller than it is. Ralph T. King, vice president of Realty Investment Company, was the first owner. The house was built in 1928—very late for Euclid Golf. (Author photograph.)

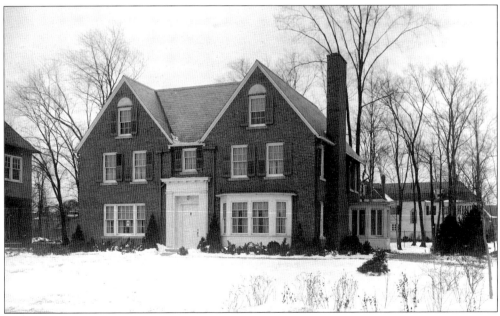

In 1917, Deming built 2225 Delamere Drive for Redge F. Henn, a relative of the founders of The National Acme Co, manufacturers of machine tools. The distinguishing feature of this Howell & Thomas design is its dramatic parallel gables punctuated by third floor windows with blind arch detailing. Notice the semi-hexagonal one storey bay on the right side of the façade and the semi-octagonal bay on the side of the house. This photograph is dated January 1918. (RSA.).

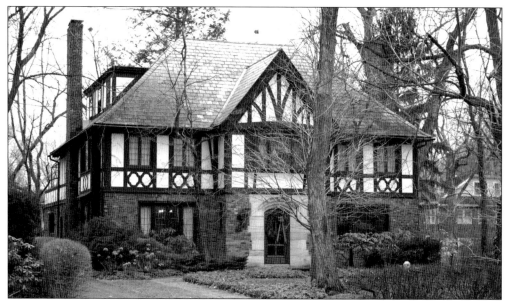

This masterful Tudor-inspired house at 2236 Demington Drive was designed by Boston architect Charles R. Greco. Greco designed a number of houses in Cleveland Heights and Shaker Heights, in addition to the Temple at East 105th Street and the Temple on the Heights. The original owner was David G. Skall, of David G. Skall Company Investments. The house was built in 1924. (Author photograph.)

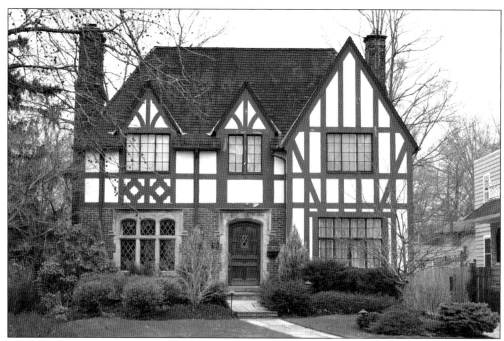

Architect Harold O. Fullerton designed this house at 2691 Scarborough Road in 1927. The original owner was William H. Ramsey, an accountant. Fullerton's houses can be found in Cleveland Heights and Shaker Heights, but he is perhaps best known for designing the Belgian Village town houses on Fairhill Road. (Author photograph.)

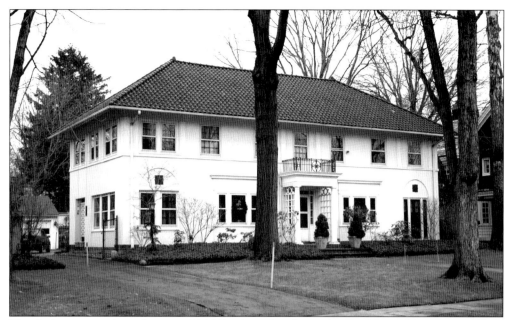

This Italian-inspired residence at 2345 Roxboro Road was designed by architect Reynold H. Hinsdale, who designed several other Euclid Golf houses. The side of the house to the left in the picture was originally an open porch with a sleeping porch above. Builder H.L. Haines advertised the house in *Town Topics* on November 13, 1920, for $45,000. (Author photograph.)

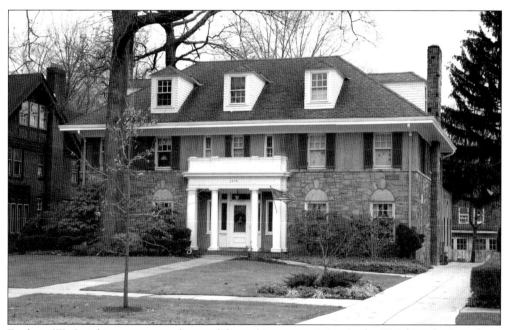

Frederic W. Striebinger was another prolific architect practicing in the Heights who is perhaps best known for his Beaux Arts style Tremaine-Gallagher house on Fairmount Boulevard. One of the houses he designed in Euclid Golf is this at 2274 Demington Drive. This eclectic Colonial was originally owned by William C. Talmage and was constructed in 1922 by builder Benjamin C. Hinig. (Author photograph.)

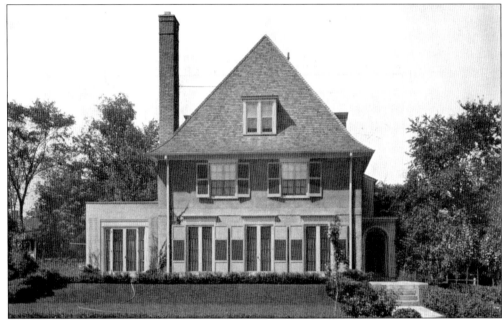

William B. Cockley, whose house at 2220 Woodmere Drive was built by Deming in 1918, was a lawyer with the firm Tolles, Hogsett & Ginn. Howell & Thomas designed a French-inspired house in stucco with French doors on the first storey and a steeply pitched hipped roof with flared eves. The entrance is on the right side of the house, and a flat roofed sun porch is on the left side. This photograph is from Deming's later brochure. (Weston Schmitt.)

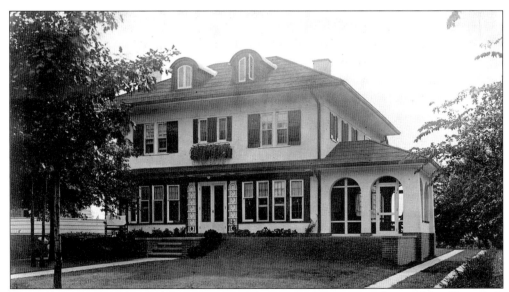

This eclectic Italian-inspired house at 2346 Demington Drive was designed by Howell & Thomas and built by Deming in 1916. While the body of the house is stucco, bowed windows dominate the first storey. Arches in the side porch mirror the round-topped dormers in the hipped roof. The deep eves would usually be bracketed in Italian Renaissance architecture. First owner Walter A. Green was treasurer of the Colonnade Company, a restaurant chain. This photograph is dated August 1916. (RSA.)

*Five*

# PROMINENT PEOPLE OF EUCLID GOLF

Just six years after Deming began development of Euclid Golf, he referred to Fairmount Boulevard as "The Euclid Avenue of the Heights." Again in a 1920 advertisement, Deming expounded upon the idea: "The splendid neighborhood at Ardleigh Drive and Delamere Drive in the Euclid Golf development, where these beautiful streets intersect with Fairmount Boulevard, has naturally, by virtue of just its location, become the home site for many of Cleveland's first families."

We know about some of these homeowners from an article in the May 1921 issue of *The Architectural Forum*. The article recognizes Euclid Golf as an outstanding example of suburban real estate development. It praises the B.R. Deming Company and Howell & Thomas Architects for creating a residential community that is both architecturally pleasing and financially successful. "To [Clevelanders]," it says, "[Euclid Golf] signifies a district centering about a wide curved boulevard, crossed by a dozen or so winding streets of generous width, an abundance of fine old trees and a sprinkling of substantial houses which are, as suburban houses go, quite likely in size and character."

The article shows photographs and floor plans for 11 Euclid Golf homes designed by Howell & Thomas. Three of the homes are Fairmount Boulevard mansions, while the rest are more modest side street domains. The homes include those of A.C. Ernst, Esq., founding partner of Ernst & Ernst Accountants (2540 Fairmount); Mr. Thomas H. White, son of the founder of White Motors Company (2335 Delamere); and Charles A. Forster, president of the Packard Cleveland Motor Company (2231 Delamere).

As Cleveland's elite changed their addresses from Euclid Avenue to the Heights, they filled their new homes with the latest in early twentieth-century technology and conveniences. Many houses used Mouat Vapor Heat, Kernerator built-in-the-chimney incinerators, and "Minneapolis" heat regulators. Some houses featured fireproof steel frames. In keeping with the latest ideas about sanitation, many homes had tiled kitchens.

Euclid Golf homes also reflected the changing social patterns of the early twentieth century. Compared to those of Euclid Avenue, Euclid Golf homes were more horizontal and in closer relation with each other and the street. Lots were large enough for gardens and ornamental plantings, but not so big as to be impractical. Victorian formality was giving way to more open floor plans. Few Euclid Golf homes contained elaborate ballrooms. Instead, they featured dining rooms, living rooms, libraries, and dens meant for more intimate gatherings.

The increasing popularity of the automobile can be seen in Euclid Golf homes. While homes built before 1919 had detached garages at the rear of the property, homes built later generally had attached ones (although they were still to the rear of the house). The importance of the outdoors to the suburban ideal is evident in the garden rooms, porches, and patios that integrate the interior of the house with the surrounding landscape. Elaborate garden layouts decorated with ornaments, pergola, fountains, and pools have the effect of creating outdoor rooms. Euclid Golf homes were built to take advantage of the abundant unskilled labor force available for domestic service. Sleeping rooms for live-in help were connected via back staircases to the kitchens, pantries, storage rooms, and garages where the daily chores of domestic life were accomplished.

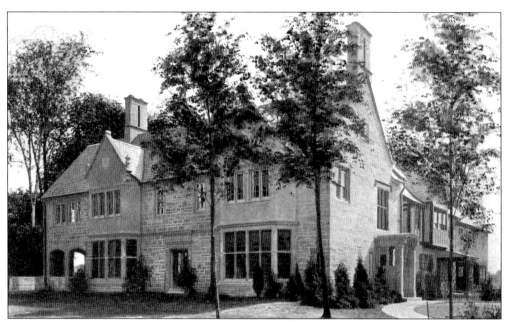

The first owner of 2540 Fairmount Boulevard, Alwyn C. Ernst, was the founding partner of Ernst & Ernst, a forerunner in accounting and management consulting. His firm later became Ernst & Whinney, and today is Ernst & Young. Deming began construction of this Howell & Thomas design on speculation, and the house was nearly complete when Ernst purchased it. The stone Lutyens-styled Tudor Revival house was completed in 1920. Not surprisingly, Deming prominently featured the house in his later brochure. (Weston Schmitt.)

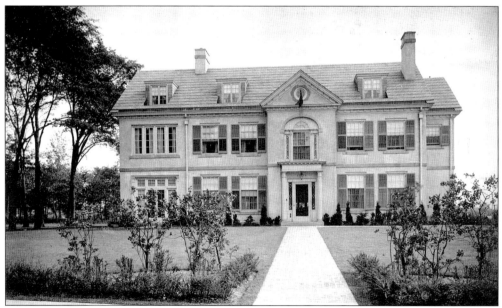

One of the showcases of Euclid Golf is this lovely Colonial Revival at 2574 Fairmount Boulevard designed by Howell & Thomas. Built on speculation by Deming in 1916, its first owner was Julia Harkness York, widow of Barney H. York. The Yorks originally lived on Euclid Avenue and were a part of Avenue society. This photograph is dated June 1917. (RSA.)

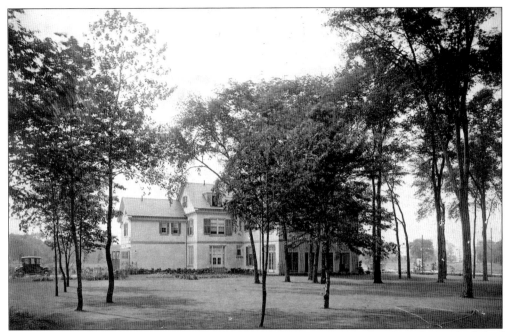

This photograph shows 2574 Fairmount Boulevard again, this time from the side. To the left of the photograph is an electric powered automobile in front of the open doors of the attached garage. Notice to the right of the photograph the as-yet undeveloped land. This photograph is dated June 1917. (RSA.)

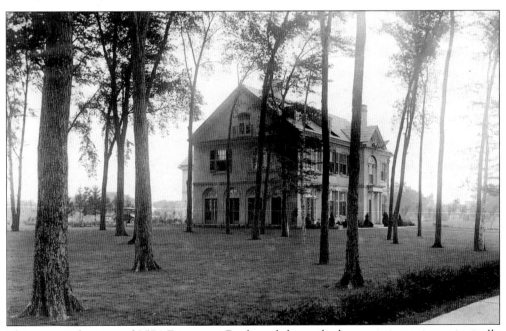

This spectacular view of 2574 Fairmount Boulevard shows the house sitting quite majestically all alone on this stretch of Fairmount. Deming intended for this house to be a showcase for Fairmount Boulevard, and we think he and Howell & Thomas succeeded! This photograph is dated June 1917. (RSA.)

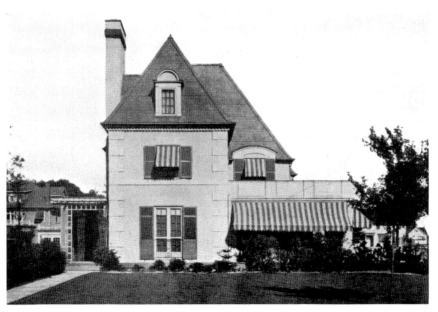

HOUSE OF THOMAS WHITE, Esquire
2335 DELAMERE DRIVE, EUCLID GOLF

*Howell & Thomas, Architects*

# MOUAT VAPOR HEAT

*Some of the fine homes illustrated in this
book equipped with MOUAT HEAT*

A. C. Ernst Residence
B. R. Deming Residence
Mrs. B. H. York Residence
R. G. Pack Residence
Euclid Golf Allotment House No. 190
Roland White Residence
Euclid Golf Allotment House No. 7
(Coventry Road Near Fairmount Boulevard)

## THE MOUAT-SQUIRES CO.

1246 WEST FOURTH STREET

CLEVELAND

The French-inspired house featured in this advertisement for Mouat Vapor Heat products is that of Thomas Holden White and his wife Kathleen York White. White was the son of Windsor T. White of White Motors and White Sewing Machine. This house at 2335 Delamere Drive was designed by Howell & Thomas and built by Deming on speculation in 1917. The advertisement is from Deming's later brochure. (Weston Schmitt.)

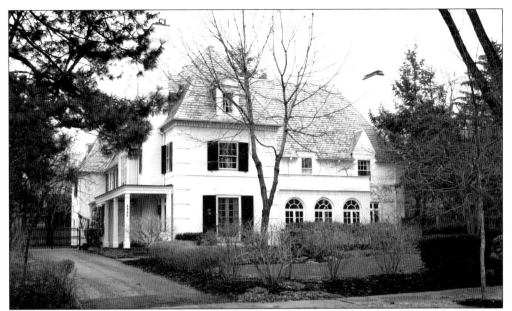

In 1929, Thomas H. White had Howell & Thomas design a massive addition to his house at 2335 Delamere Drive (see previous page). More than doubling the size of the house, the addition also dramatically changes the home's massing and its street presentation. (Author photograph.)

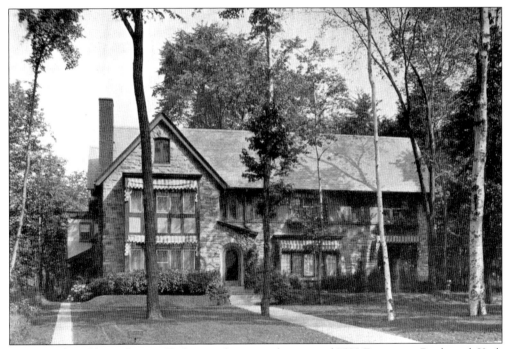

Roy F. York and his wife Mary York were the original owners of 2583 Fairmount Boulevard. York was president of Stearns Motor Sales and the son of Julia York, who lived across the street at 2574 Fairmount (page 88). Later, the house was owned by another former Euclid Avenue resident, Anne Treadway, the widow of Lyman Treadway. This English inspired house was designed by Howell & Thomas and built by Deming between 1916 and 1917. (Weston Schmitt.)

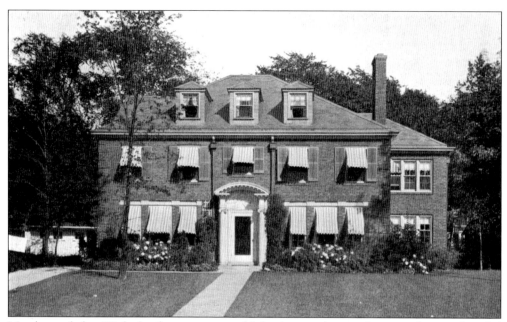

Members of the Wick family were successful bankers and manufacturers, having founded National City Bank and Republic Iron Works, later Republic Steel, among other companies. Kenneth B. Wick, the owner of 2259 Delamere Drive, was the treasurer of the Wick Investment Company. Deming built this Howell & Thomas designed house in 1917. (Weston Schmitt.)

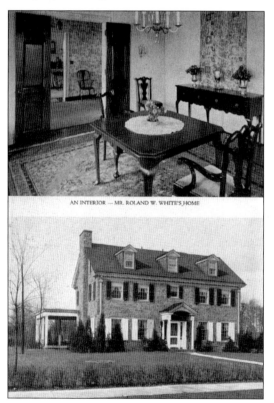

AN INTERIOR — MR. ROLAND W. WHITE'S HOME

Deming built this stone house at 2222 Delamere Drive in 1919 for Roland W. White, who was the president of the Colonnade Company, a well-known chain of restaurants. The house was designed by Howell & Thomas. Deming featured the house in his later brochure and included a view of White's dining room. (Weston Schmitt.)

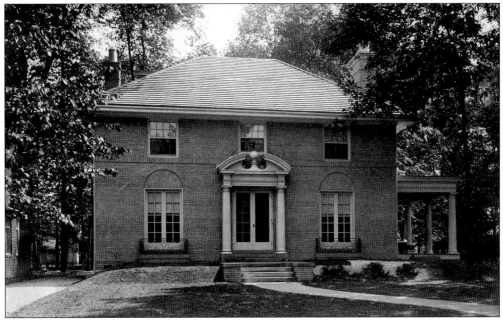

This lovely Italian-inspired residence at 2243 Tudor Drive was the home of Murlan J. Murphy, president of the Phoenix Oil Company. Murphy's father, Jeremiah T. Murphy, was responsible for bringing Murphy's Oil Soap to market. This house was designed by Gustave B. Bohm and was featured in the December 1916 edition of *Ohio Architect, Engineer and Builder*. Note the remarkable broken pediment and the delicate ironwork. The photograph was taken *c*. 1916. (RSA.)

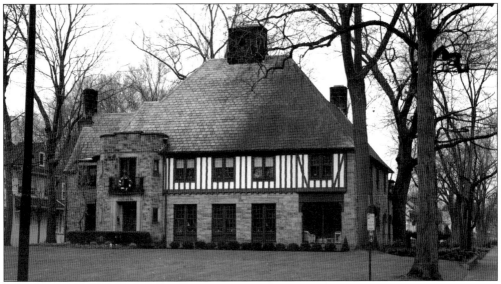

2638 Fairmount Boulevard was designed by the prolific firm Walker & Weeks for Armen Tashjian, the firm's chief engineer. Tashjian was born in Armenia and attended Yale and MIT. He was known nationally for inventing a reinforced steel used in bank vaults, and his engineering skills were key in many Walker & Weeks projects, including the Federal Reserve Bank of Cleveland. Pink granite tiles on the rear terrace are the same material used for the Federal Reserve. (Author photograph.)

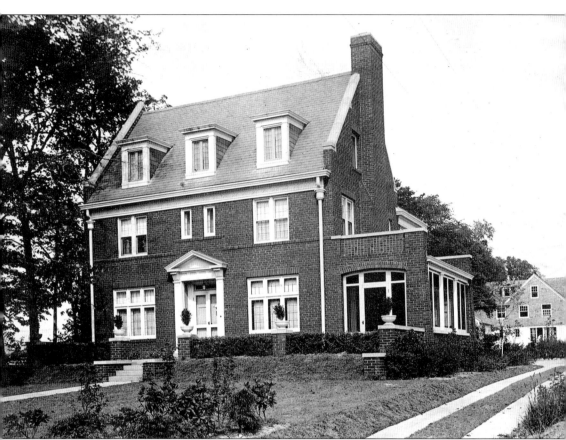

This lovely house at 2277 Chatfield, designed by Howell & Thomas, features a double-door entrance with a classical pediment, leaded glass windows, and stone-capped parapeted gables. Deming completed the house in 1916 for Dr. Aladar and Bertha Pacz. Dr. Pacz, from Hungary, was a scientist with General Electric who invented a non-sag tungsten filament material that revolutionized the incandescent lamp. Between 1908 and 1933, Pacz was granted 46 U.S. patents. This photograph is dated July 1916. (RSA.)

# Six

# MARKETING EUCLID GOLF

Deming advertised Euclid Golf extensively. In *Cleveland Town Topics* alone, over 175 Euclid Golf advertisements appear from 1913 to 1928. The advertisements tell the story of Euclid Golf's development and document the ups and downs of the real estate market as Deming strove to meet his sales goals. Deming's own house at the entrance to Euclid Golf served as subtle advertisement to prospective residents making their way up to the Heights from Euclid Avenue. Billboards and signs, not unlike those used by developers today, marked the other entrances to the allotment.

Deming's advertising was aggressive and extensive. He may have been the first Cleveland developer to use detailed drawings and photographs of completed spec houses to illustrate the homes in his allotment. A four-fold brochure featured a street layout and photographs of completed homes. Later, a 40-page brochure published *c.* 1921, entitled *The Euclid Golf Neighborhood*, featured the exteriors and interiors of several homes, the prominent owners of which added to the neighborhood's prestige. Deming had many photographs taken of the houses as they were completed and was successful in having articles written about Euclid Golf in such esteemed publications as *The Architectural Forum*.

As was common in the early twentieth century, many of the architectural firms who designed homes in Euclid Golf used their own builders to construct their houses. Large-scale immigration in Cleveland brought an abundant supply of skilled craftsman who masterfully executed the architects' plans. Fillous & Ruppel, architectural sculptors, provided many of the woodcarving and ornamental plasterwork in Euclid Golf. The Rose Iron Works (still in business today; 1536-40 East 43rd Street, Cleveland) provided ornamental iron and bronze work. R. Colard Wright Stained Glass supplied the leaded glass in many of the Tudor Revival homes. The B.R. Deming Company took pride in the skill and craftsmanship of both its own workmen and the suppliers with whom they worked. The skillful manipulation of natural materials such as stone, tile, slate, and wrought iron create a finely textured, aesthetically pleasing environment in Euclid Golf.

The B.R. Deming Company likewise had its own building department to construct homes on company owned lots. The construction took place under the supervision of fine residential architects, such as Howell & Thomas. This afforded Deming one more level of control in seeking to build a high-quality residential development. Many Euclid Golf purchasers chose the B.R. Deming Company to build their homes, which were referred to as "Deming-built." The company boasted of their "carefully chosen materials and directly employed workmen, under the supervision of [their] own building experts." As an astute businessman, Deming also sought to promote customer satisfaction and limit construction costs.

The extent to which B.R. Deming desired to protect his allotment from undesirable influences is shown by his purchase of three lots on the south side of West St. James Parkway from another developer and the design of pleasing houses to block the unsightly view of "a poor class of investment houses with no restrictions." Mr. Howell designed number 2600, Mr. Thomas designed number 2594, and they both designed a double house, number 2580-82, at the boundary of the allotment on West St. James Parkway. These three houses, though not technically part of Euclid Golf, are included in the historic district because of their high-quality design and construction and their unique role in protecting Euclid Golf.

Deming ran this advertisement for Euclid Golf in the October 18, 1913, edition of *Cleveland Town Topics,* the society weekly of the day. This would be the first of over 175 such advertisements Deming would place in this publication alone. Deming placed a large advertisement for Euclid Golf as early as May 11, 1913, in *The Cleveland Leader.* (The Western Reserve Historical Society, Cleveland, Ohio.)

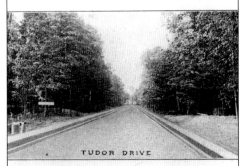

# EUCLID GOLF

**TUDOR DRIVE**

LOTS in Euclid Golf Allotment are the most desirable home sites on the Heights. Located virtually at the entrance to the Heights residential district, Euclid Golf residents are within six minutes' car ride of East 105th street and Euclid avenue.

The natural beauty of this property suggests and demands the upbuilding of a community of homes of refinement and character. Our Architectural and Building departments are giving the same careful study to the architectural and artistic features of the inexpensive home as to the most pretentious boulevard residence. The wooded parts of Euclid Golf lend themselves particularly to individual treatment.

Building can be started this fall and your home will be ready for occupancy in the spring.

*Lots $2200 to $7800*

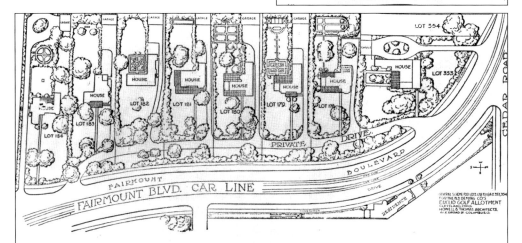

# *The Euclid Golf Residential Section*

The illustration shows the proposed development of the lots on either side of Fairmount Blvd., just east of Cedar Rd. One of these houses has been built as suggested. This section is located on a high cliff and affords a beautiful view of the surroundings, it being possible to see Lake Erie on a clear day. The most beautiful trees in Euclid Golf are on these lots.

| LOTS | HOUSES |
|---|---|
| This is but an example of the manner in which the new EUCLID GOLF residential section is being developed by The B. R. Deming Co. The large deep lots on Fairmount Blvd., or its tributary drives, give abundant opportunity for residence work of merit. Lots $49 to $100 per foot, with all improvements included in the price. | Our Building Dept. is prepared to take over the complete handling of your house from drawing the plans to building the house —from excavation to interior finish—under the close supervision of practical builders and architects. The office is prepared to show sketches and plans of charming homes. Make your appointment with the office to see this property. Phone Doan 2411. |

This September 26, 1914, *Town Topics* advertisement features a plan for the lots along Fairmount Boulevard beginning at Cedar Road. This would be the only portion of Euclid Golf not realized as planned. The Heights Medical Arts Building occupies lots 353 and 354, and lots 178 through 180 were never developed. (The Western Reserve Historical Society, Cleveland, Ohio.)

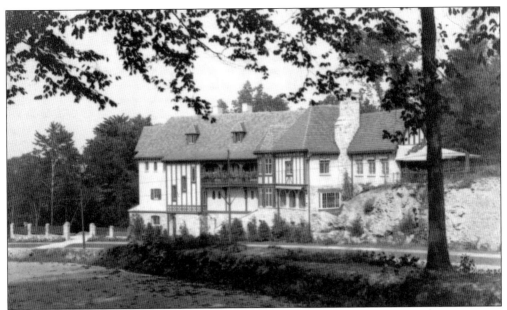

No discussion of the marketing of Euclid Golf would be complete without a mention of Deming's own house. Deming charged his architects, Howell & Thomas, to design a house that would act as a billboard that proclaimed the beauty and grandeur of Euclid Golf. This particular advertisement was completed in 1914. (RSA.)

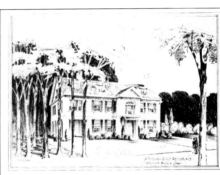

*A Residence on Fairmount Boulevard, near Delamere Drive*

## Delamere Drive
### IN THE
## Euclid Golf Neighborhood

DELAMERE DRIVE is so laid out as to make it one of the finest and most exclusive small streets on the heights. Lots vary in depth from 200 to 215 feet and are 80 and 90 feet in width. If your happiness needs flowers, shrubbery and beautiful hedges, the west side of the street has ideal exposure for your garden. If a background of stately trees is more to your liking the east side of Delamere Drive will appeal to you.

We consider this group of Delamere lots to be one of the choicest community settings in our neighborhood. Since last week several additional lots have been sold on this street leaving a little more than half of the lots still available. It will pay you to buy your lot now.

Like all other parts of the Euclid Golf Neighborhood, residents of Delamere Drive have the advantage of frequent car service and a general accessibility to the activities of the entire family that is so necessary to the ideal location.

Wm B.R. Deming Co.

*"Developers of the Euclid Golf Neighborhood and Builders of Homes in that Community"*
*513 Cuyahoga Building*

This December 9, 1916, *Town Topics* advertisement describes Delamere Drive as "one of the finest and most exclusive small streets on the heights." Curiously, Deming chose to illustrate his point by featuring Howell & Thomas' drawing of 2574 Fairmount, built around the corner from Delamere Drive. (The Western Reserve Historical Society, Cleveland, Ohio.)

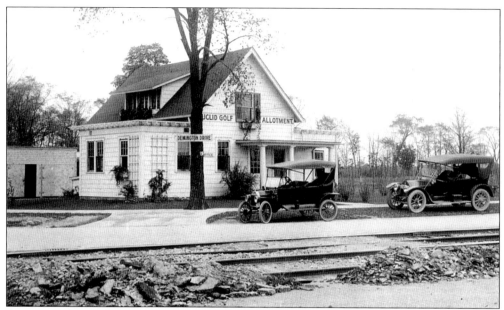

Deming understood the importance of presentation, particularly in selling land and houses to an upscale purchaser. Consequently, his allotment office at Fairmount Boulevard and Demington Drive, with its window boxes and trellises, reflects the picturesque qualities he claimed for the entire allotment. (RSA.)

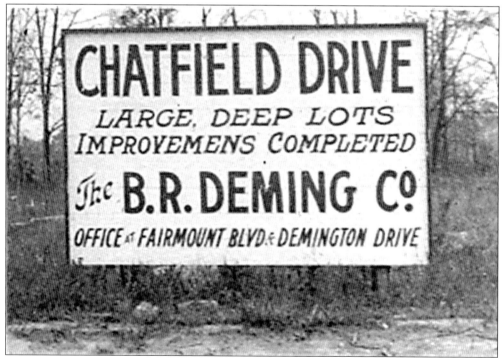

Deming was quick to capitalize upon the continuous streetcar traffic passing through Euclid Golf by erecting large billboards at the foot of each sidestreet off of Fairmount Boulevard. The signs describe the features of the lots on each street. (RSA.)

This March 3, 1917, *Town Topics* advertisement describes the initial development of the side streets south of Fairmount Boulevard. Note also the description of the appreciation of land values in the short time Euclid Golf has been under development. (The Western Reserve Historical Society, Cleveland, Ohio.)

# THREE NEW STREETS
IN
## The Euclid Golf Neighborhood
### Roxboro Road
### Tudor Drive          Delamere Drive
(South of Fairmount Blvd.)

THIS part of the *Euclid Golf* neighborhood is now being actively marketed for the first time. We have delayed operations south of Fairmount Blvd. until other parts of the *Euclid Golf* neighborhood were firmly established. This section will now be built up in just as high grade manner as that part of *Euclid Golf* north of the Boulevard.

Two of the finest homes on the Heights have been built on Fairmount Blvd. adjacent to these side streets. We have already started the construction, in this section, of a residence, which, when completed, will sell for approximately $21,000. Plans for others of a similar character are under way and building will soon commence.

### A COMPARISON OF VALUES

OF 116 lots located on side streets, north of Fairmount Boulevard, we have unsold 20 scattered lots. This property first sold at prices ranging from $47.50 to $50 per ft. The majority of recent sales have been around $65 to $70 per ft.

Property on Tudor, Roxboro and Delamere, south of Fairmount Blvd., is placed on the market at an average of $55.00 per ft. We ourselves are setting the standard of development. The development will not only be as good or better in quality than we have already done in *Euclid Golf*, but it will be more rapid.

Communicate with our Sales Department.

*The B. R. Deming Co.*

Office: 513 Cuyahoga Bldg.          Main 5530 or Garfield 2411

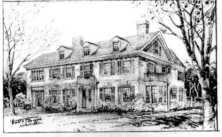

## *The*
## EUCLID GOLF NEIGHBORHOOD

### *Brick Residence Being Built For Sale on Fairmount Blvd.*

THIS brick colonial residence is now under construction on one of the most beautiful lots on Fairmount Blvd. The style of the house reflects the colonial architecture found in the neighborhood of Philadelphia and Germantown—dignified and substantial—yet expressing the most homelike and hospitable air.

The entrance to the house is thru a broad recessed entrance—panelled in white—into a large center hall with colonial stairway. The hall runs straight thru the house ending on another broad recessed stoop—giving an outlook into the garden spot.

On one side is a large living room, with glass enclosed porch off one side and connecting with comfortable library to the rear—broad open fire-places in both living room and library. The dining room is featured with a large semi-circular glass bay at one end—large enough to place a moderate sized table for informal use. Kitchen, pantry and general service equipment are complete and practical. Second floor has four very large bed rooms, sleeping porch, dressing room, and two baths. Third floor has maids' rooms, bath and storage space.

The lot is 100x335 and has a number of large trees in excellent condition. This home is in keeping with others we have erected and the economy we are practicing in its development makes the price at which it will sell less than what it would cost an individual to build a similar place for himself.

*Communicate with our Sales Department.*

*The B. R. Deming Co.*

Office, 513 Cuyahoga Bldg.          Main 5530—Garf. 2411

Construction of 2520 Fairmount Boulevard had barely begun when Deming advertised the house in the May 19, 1917, edition of *Town Topics*. The ad copy describes the features and plan of the house, backed up by Howell & Thomas' rendering. (The Western Reserve Historical Society, Cleveland, Ohio.)

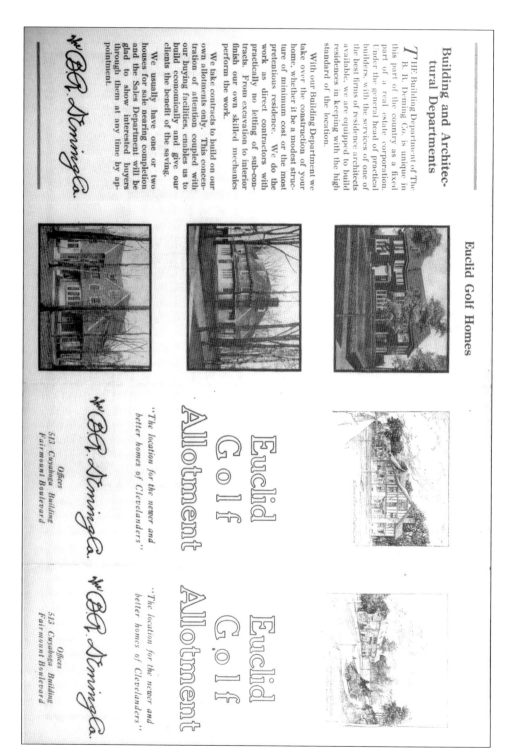

## Building and Architectural Departments

*T*HE Building Department of The B. R. Deming Co. is unique in this part of the country as a fixed part of a real estate corporation. Under the general head of practical builders, with the services of one of the best firms of residence architects available, we are equipped to build residences in keeping with the high standard of the location.

With our Building Department we take over the construction of your home, whether it be a modest structure of minimum cost or the most pretentious residence. We do the work as direct contractors with practically no letting of sub-contracts. From excavation to interior finish our own skilled mechanics perform the work.

We take contracts to build on our own allotments only. This concentration of attention coupled with our buying facilities, enables us to build economically and give our clients the benefit of the saving.

We usually have one or two houses for sale nearing completion and the Sales Department will be glad to show interested buyers through them at any time by appointment.

*The* B. R. Deming Co.

**Euclid Golf Homes**

*"The location for the newer and better homes of Clevelanders"*

## Euclid Golf Allotment

Offices
513 Cuyahoga Building
Fairmount Boulevard

*The* B. R. Deming Co.

*"The location for the newer and better homes of Clevelanders"*

## Euclid Golf Allotment

Offices
513 Cuyahoga Building
Fairmount Boulevard

*The* B. R. Deming Co.

Around 1916, Deming published his first of two brochures. This was a four-fold brochure illustrated with photographs of completed houses and drawings of street scenes. (The Western Reserve Historical Society, Cleveland, Ohio.)

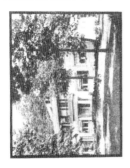
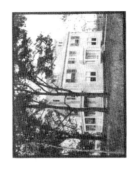
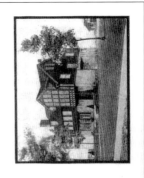

# Some Euclid Golf Homes

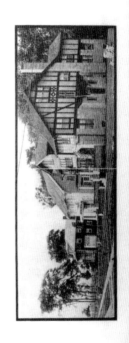

## The Euclid Golf Neighborhood

*I*N PURCHASING a home in Euclid Golf you do more than purchase a mere piece of land of great natural beauty, furnished with high grade permanent improvements, and so located as to street car service and general accessibility as to make it the most convenient location for a home in Cleveland. You get all that in Euclid Golf and you get something far more valuable.

You get a share in a neighborhood interest that is expressed in well kept lawns, tastefully treated homes, a general wholesome neighborliness and pride in community that is enthusiastic, spontaneous and sincere. It is this intangible yet noticeable atmosphere of neighborhood interest, which even the stranger feels in driving through the streets that makes Euclid Golf the place where more and more Clevelanders of culture and refinement want to make their homes.

## The B. R. Deming Co.

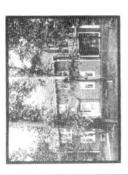
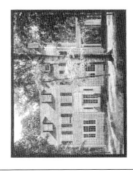
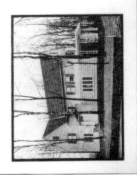

This is the reverse of the *c.* 1916 brochure, featuring more photographs of completed houses. The interior of the brochure contains the allotment map complete with street layouts and lot numbers. (The Western Reserve Historical Society, Cleveland, Ohio.)

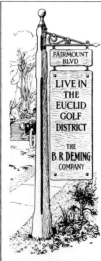

# EUCLID GOLF

*The property that is not too far out nor too close in*

**A SAFE INVESTMENT TODAY, TOMORROW AND ALWAYS**

This is a fact because of the carefully guarded restrictions and the class of homes already erected. If the future of Euclid Golf neighborhood may be judged by present accomplishment now so well and favorably known, an investment in your future home site is absolutely safe and the wisdom of obtaining it now is without question. The number of Euclid Golf lots is limited and when sold there will be no more as well located because Euclid Golf is the best located residential Heights property where the particular home builder is amply protected in point of restrictions and neighbors. With normal conditions and reach assured the wise man will be forehanded and buy now and prepare to build.

### Our Sales Department

have a number of residences in Euclid Golf for sale at prices from $18,000 up.

*The BR Deming Co*

*Office: Corner Fairmount Boulevard and Demington Drive*

This November 16, 1918, *Town Topics* advertisement points out to prospective buyers that their investment in Euclid Golf is a safe one due to careful planning and deed restrictions. While the iron work on the street sign in the illustration is similar to those originally installed in Euclid Golf, the carved post is not. (The Western Reserve Historical Society, Cleveland, Ohio.)

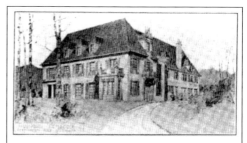

THIS individual and attractive home is influenced by French Architecture. It is the second of a series of proposed houses for Fairmount Boulevard in

### EUCLID GOLF

The floor arrangement of this house may be seen by applying at our office. Two other houses may be inspected at any time. Both of them reflect the high standard of excellence maintained by our building department.

If not a house, EUCLID GOLF has the finest residential lots on the Heights.

*The BR Deming Co*

**REALTORS**

*Fairmount Blvd. and Demington Drive*

Fairmount 473

The house featured in this April 5, 1919, *Town Topics* advertisement was not actually built. Based upon the massing and fenestration of this design, we suspect that this was a French version of the English house actually built at Fairmount Boulevard and Ardleigh Drive and owned originally by A.C. Ernst. The original pencil on paper drawing used in this advertisement still exists and is in the author's collection. (The Western Reserve Historical Society, Cleveland, Ohio.)

Deming built a double house and two cottages at the foot of Tudor Drive specifically to block the view of a "less desirable" housing allotment next to Euclid Golf. None of these three Howell & Thomas houses are actually in Euclid Golf proper and are further evidence of Deming carefully protecting the values of Euclid Golf properties. This November 29, 1919 advertisement from *Town Topics* features the double house. (The Western Reserve Historical Society, Cleveland, Ohio.)

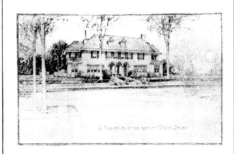

## THE FINEST DOUBLE HOUSE IN GREATER CLEVELAND FOR SALE

This house overlooks Euclid Golf, and sits squarely across Tudor Drive, looking to Fairmount Boulevard one block away. Designed by Howell & Thomas, Architects.

Two complete private homes. Each side contains seven rooms, reception hall, baths, maids' quarters with bath, two enclosed living porches. Four-part brick garage detached. Grounds being heavily planted by this Company. Shown at any time.

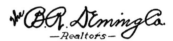

*Fairmount Blvd. and Demington Drive*
505 Bangor Bldg., 942 Prospect Avenue

Fairmount 473                    Prospect 1005

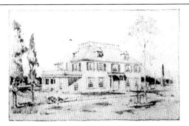

Colonial House reminiscent of old work around Salem.
FOR SALE

# IN EUCLID GOLF

This house is dignified by its purity and simplicity of lines. Well along toward completion, and will be shortly ready for occupancy. On Tudor Drive.

Spacious living room, very conveniently arranged dining room, butler's pantry, kitchen, and cold room. Open living porch; also closed living porch, which may be used for either breakfast room or library.

Four chambers, two baths, and sleeping porch on second floor.

Ample service quarters, consisting of two maids' rooms, bath, and adequate storage.

Very practical house, but losing none of its charm thereby. Finish in ivory enamel. Two-part garage. Vapor heat.

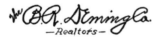

*Fairmount Blvd. and Demington Drive*
505 Bangor Bldg., 942 Prospect Avenue
Fairmount 473                    Prospect 1005

2347 Tudor Drive was built by Deming in 1919 and was advertised in *Town Topics* various times, including this ad in the August 30, 1919 edition. Howell & Thomas designed this Colonial house. (The Western Reserve Historical Society, Cleveland, Ohio.)

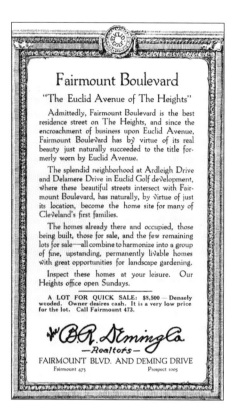

This June 12, 1920, advertisement in *Town Topics* proclaims Fairmount Boulevard to be the "Euclid Avenue of The Heights," and indeed goes on to suggest that Fairmount has replaced Euclid Avenue as the finest street for Cleveland's most prominent families. (The Western Reserve Historical Society, Cleveland, Ohio.)

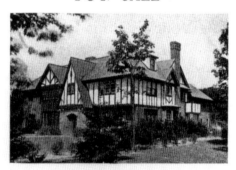

2675 Fairmount Boulevard was constructed on speculation by builder William Cunningham in 1924 and advertised nationally. *The Cleveland Heights Dispatch* described the house as "the most advertised residence in the country" and likened its construction to that of a skyscraper with its steel beams and concrete floors covered in wood. The inclusion of an elevator, intercoms, and sumptuous woodwork pushed the asking price to $200,000. The architect is Reynold H. Hinsdale. (The Western Reserve Historical Society, Cleveland, Ohio.)

# A NEW FAIRMOUNT BLVD. HOME

### FAIRMOUNT BOULEVARD AND DELAMERE DRIVE

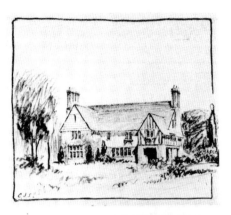

This new English Type of Brick and Timber Home is another example of the superior Residential building of Ray C. Jones, Builder. In addition to the genuine worth of construction and architectural plan, this new home has the equally important asset of situation in a group of outstanding fine residences. ⌐, A simple, yet complete and dignified plan, set off by the charm of such details as stairway, mantels, tile work and the English-made metal casements.

Ray C. Jones was a prolific builder who constructed houses of all sizes in Euclid Golf, including a number of large Fairmount Boulevard houses such as this at 2558 Fairmount. The architect for this Tudor inspired residence is Charles S. Schneider, one of Cleveland's most talented architects who is best known for having designed Stan Hywet Hall in Akron. (The Western Reserve Historical Society, Cleveland, Ohio.)

Another Ray C. Jones built house is this at 2514 Fairmount Boulevard. Its original owners were Calvin and Elizabeth Lohmiller. Lohmiller was a vice president of the Hunkin Conkey Construction Company. Built in 1925, this classically designed Georgian Revival house features early Art Deco style features on the interior. A.B. Smythe realtors advertised the house in this November 28, 1925 *Town Topics* ad. (The Western Reserve Historical Society, Cleveland, Ohio.)

### Presenting a New Georgian Residence of Exquisite Proportion

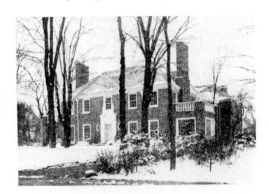

*On the Upper Drive        -        2514 Fairmount Blvd.*

Architects, builders, and the few who have been privileged to view this house, unite in pronouncing it to be one of the masterpieces of fine residence work in Cleveland. It is rich in dignity, faultless in proportion and balance, and endowed with an unmistakable air of gracious hospitality.

Those eager to see this beautiful house may do so Sunday afternoon 2 to 5 o'clock, or may call E. R. Stilwell, Cedar 437, for convenient appointment.

### THE A. B. SMYTHE CO.
Superior 2500        SMYTHE BLDG.        1001 Huron Rd.

105

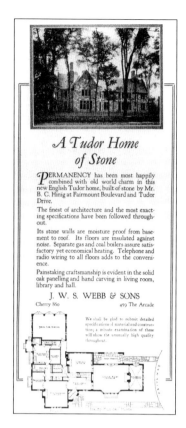

Benjamin C. Hinig was another important builder of grand Fairmount Boulevard houses, including this at 2612 Fairmount. The architect is Harold O. Fullerton. Hinig was an insurance broker and builder who, having suffered significant financial losses during the depression, jumped from the window of his Euclid Avenue office. (The Western Reserve Historical Society, Cleveland, Ohio.)

### A Tudor Home of Stone

PERMANENCY has been most happily combined with old world charm in this new English Tudor home, built of stone by Mr. B. C. Hinig at Fairmount Boulevard and Tudor Drive.

The finest of architecture and the most exacting specifications have been followed throughout.

Its stone walls are moisture proof from basement to roof. Its floors are insulated against noise. Separate gas and coal boilers assure satisfactory yet economical heating. Telephone and radio wiring to all floors adds to the convenience.

Painstaking craftsmanship is evident in the solid oak panelling and hand carving in living room, library and hall.

J. W. S. WEBB & SONS

Cherry 860                    459 The Arcade

We shall be glad to submit detailed specifications of material and construction; a minute examination of these will show the unusually high quality throughout.

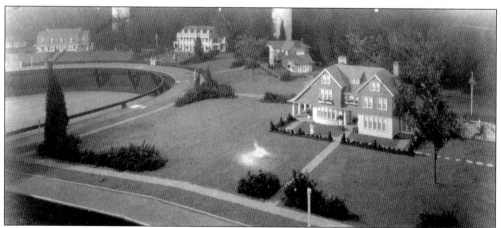

In 1916, Deming participated in the Cleveland Building Show by mounting an extraordinary exhibit of model homes—that is, exact scale replicas of Howell & Thomas designed houses! In all, nine fully detailed replicas were painstakingly constructed and presented with full garden landscaping. The exhibit was made in conjunction with the Cleveland Lumber Dealers Association to illustrate the uses of wood in home construction. The railing around the exhibit shows the scale of these models. (Thomas Family.)

106

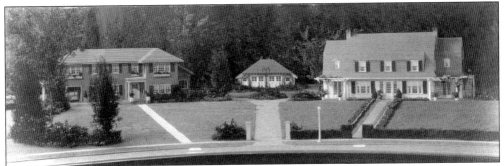

These two houses from the Cleveland Building Show feature a "two family" garage. Here, the designers envisioned a garage that would be shared by two houses, increasing the garden space around the homes. Deming and Howell & Thomas would actually employ this design feature in Euclid Golf. (See page 76.) (Thomas Family.)

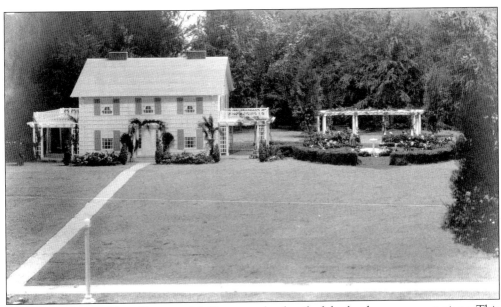

This Cleveland Building Show model illustrates the detail of the landscape presentations. This house features climbing vines, hedges, flower borders, and a garden fountain. Structures such as the fully trellised façade, pergola front entrance, and the large garden pergola exemplify the then-current interest in linking architecture to the landscape. Albert D. Taylor is the landscape architect for the exhibit. (Thomas Family.)

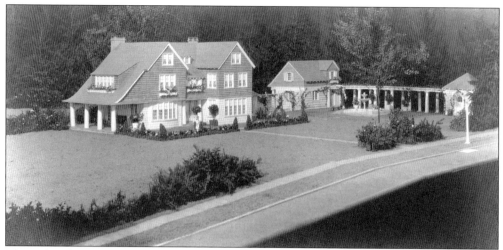

This Cleveland Building Show model features an extensive curved garden pergola and garden house. While these two elements were not actually built, the house was built by Deming for Ernest W. Whittemore at 2270 Tudor Drive in 1915 (see below). The Deming exhibit at the Cleveland Building Show was extensively covered complete with photographs and floorplans in the December 1916 edition of *The Ohio Architect, Engineer and Builder*. (Thomas Family.)

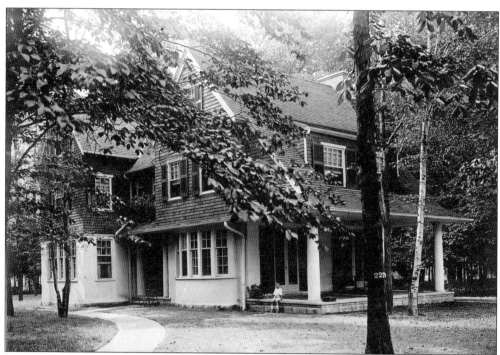

Howell & Thomas designed this house at 2270 Tudor Drive for Ernest W. Whittemore. Built by Deming in 1915, this Shingle style house is situated such that its side porch is facing the street, rather different than the site plan featured in the Cleveland Building Show above. Note the youngster sitting on the edge of the porch in the photograph. Whittemore was treasurer of National Malleable Castings Company. This photograph is dated July 1916. (RSA.)

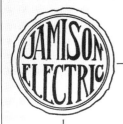

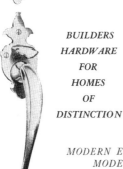
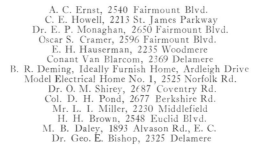
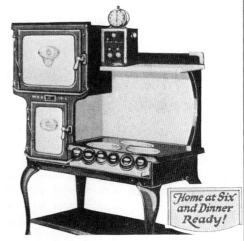
The Jamison Electric Company did electrical wiring, as well as sold decorative hardware and appliances, such as this Westinghouse range. Jamison was one of the advertisers in Deming's later brochure. Note the Euclid Golf addresses where Jamison did work. (City of Cleveland Heights.)

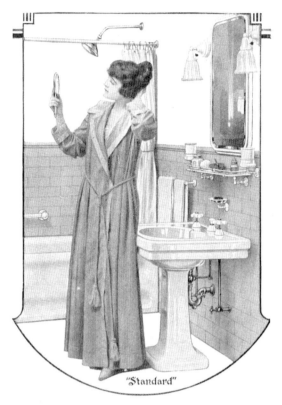

"Standard"

The Plumbing and Heating in Many
of the Residences in the
## Euclid Golf District
Illustrated in this Publication were
Installed by
# J. L. Croft & Co.
Estimates Cheerfully Furnished, Repair
Work Promptly Attended To
## Cleveland

J.L. Croft and Company was another contractor who advertised in Deming's brochure. Croft was a plumbing and heating contractor who did work in Euclid Golf. (City of Cleveland Heights.)

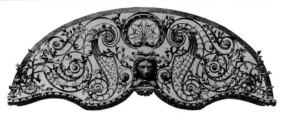
The Rose Iron Works provided decorative iron work for many Euclid Golf houses and advertised in Deming's brochure. Examples of Rose Iron Works' handiwork can be found throughout the Cleveland area, and they remain in business to this day. (City of Cleveland Heights.)

The Smith & Oby Company is another advertiser in Deming's brochure. Smith & Oby is a heating and plumbing contractor and is still in business today at the same location. Note that the listing of people for whom Smith & Oby did work is a veritable Who's Who of prominent Clevelanders. (City of Cleveland Heights.)

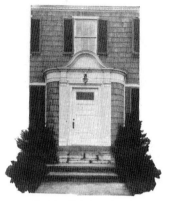

Detail of Doorway Feature

# Deming Built Homes

Carefully chosen materials and directly employed workmen, under the supervision of our own building experts, are features that make possible the quality and economy of all Deming Built houses. Many of these workmen have been with us for years and are unusually skillful in their particular branches of building.

The fact that The B. R. Deming Company was selected to build the majority of the homes in Euclid Golf, is but added evidence of our building department's superiority. The owners of these homes know that they are built **well** and **economically**. Ask any Euclid Golf resident about the all-round merits of Deming Built homes.

We are prepared to assume the entire responsibility for the building of homes from excavation to interior finish. The fact that we use only the highest class of materials and employ worth while workmen, does not necessarily mean that our bids are the highest. You are invited to consult with our Building Department—just telephone Fairmount 473 and an appointment will be arranged that will suit **your** convenience.

*The B. R. Deming Co.*

*Fairmount Boulevard and Demington Drive*

Deming himself "advertised" in his brochure, here making prospective homeowners aware that his company is capable of the complete building process, from excavation to interior finish work. The detail photograph is of the doorway of 2290 Ardleigh Drive. (City of Cleveland Heights.)

# Seven

# HOWELL & THOMAS

# ARCHITECTS

James William Thomas Jr., born in West Pittston, Pennsylvania, attended the University of Pennsylvania School of Architecture and roomed with Carl Howell. He entered a design competition for a monument, and although his design took fifth place, judge Cass Gilbert, thought so highly of his work that he invited him to work with him, and Thomas moved to New York to work under Gilbert.

Carl Eugene Howell was born in 1879. A native of Columbus, Ohio, he studied architecture at Ohio State University. He concluded his studies at the University of Pennsylvania School of Architecture and in Europe. Upon graduation, he established an office in Columbus. Several years later, he invited Thomas to come in as his partner. A perfectionist who relished the rich heritage of European design, he perhaps needed the astute business sense of his friend and former roommate.

The firm designed many outstanding buildings in Columbus, Ohio: East High School, the Library and Auditorium at Ohio State University, St. John's Episcopal Church, the Schoedinger State Street Chapel, and the tea room at the Lazarus Department Store. They designed many residences in and around Columbus, such as in the suburb of Bexley, where they designed homes for the Forest Realty Company and for prominent individuals such as Fred Lazarus, founder of Lazarus Department Stores.

Howell & Thomas established an office in Cleveland in 1914 when the B.R. Deming Company contracted them to design model homes for the Euclid Golf Allotment. One of their first commissions was B.R. Deming's own home (2485 Fairmount Boulevard). Its prominent and unusual location, at the top of an escarpment on an extremely narrow lot that contained a steep gorge, led to the distinctive structure that earned them the reputation as architects of merit.

Outside of Euclid Golf, they were commissioned for the homes of Julius Feiss and Isadore Joseph, founders of the Joseph & Feiss Company, clothiers; Will Halle, an investments broker; and Alec Printz of Printz-Bierderman Company. They designed model homes for the Van Sweringen bothers' Shaker Heights development. The firm designed schools for Lakewood and Shaker Heights; churches in Canton, Columbus, and Oxford, Ohio; YMCA buildings in Cleveland, Newark, and Zanesville; and residences and commercial buildings in many Ohio towns.

Carl Howell became ill in 1927. He retired from the firm and took a trip to the Southwest, hoping to improve his health. He died in Monrovia, California in 1930. James Thomas kept the firm going. A commission for Tom Sidlo, partner in the law firm of Baker, Hostetler & Sidlo and attorney for the *Cleveland Press*, led to the job of modernizing the Press' plant at East 9th and Rockwell. During the lean years of the Depression, the firm was able to leverage this initial work and eventually built over 20 newspaper plants all over the country.

Howell & Thomas excelled at creating their era's Revival-style homes, which were models of restraint and good taste. The interiors of their homes were comfortable and modern, while their facades were bold and interesting. Architectural periodicals of the day, such as *The Architectural Forum* and *The Ohio Architect, Engineer and Builder*, featured their work regularly. The firm's papers are now housed at the Cleveland Public Library.

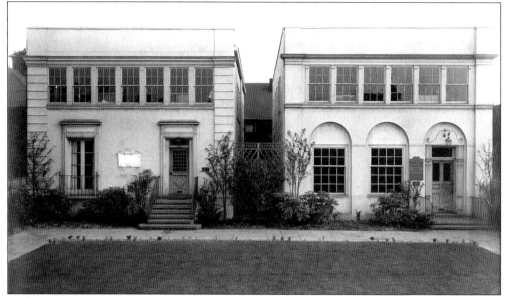

Howell & Thomas' Cleveland office was on Carnegie Avenue in a complex that also housed the offices of landscape architects William Pitkin & Seward Mott. The pair of symmetrical office buildings, still standing today, won the award for structures in their class and were featured in *Architectural Record*. Howell & Thomas also collaborated with landscape architects A.D. Taylor and A. Donald Gray, and in fact, designed Gray's home in Cleveland Heights. (Thomas Family.)

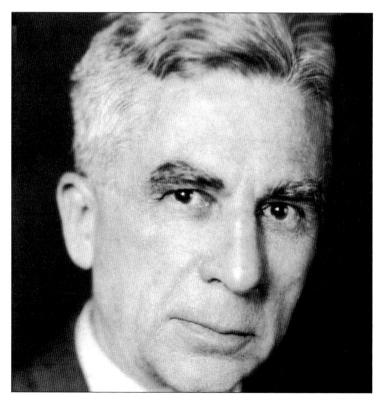

James W. Thomas in a photograph *c.* 1930. (Thomas Family.)

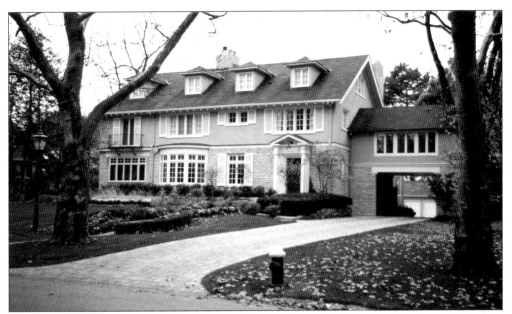

Howell & Thomas designed several houses for members of the Lazarus family in Columbus, Ohio. This house at 43 Preston Road in Bexley, Ohio, a suburb of Columbus, was designed for Robert Lazarus, vice president of the F&R Lazarus department store. The house was designed in 1924. (Author photograph.)

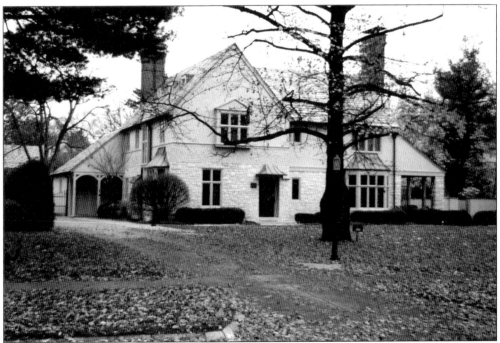

This house at 184 South Parkview in Bexley, Ohio, was designed by Howell & Thomas for Aubrey G. Lohmes, who was the secretary-treasurer of Smith Brothers Hardware. The house was built in 1923. The light colored stone on this house is indigenous to the Columbus area and is common on Bexley houses. (Author photograph.)

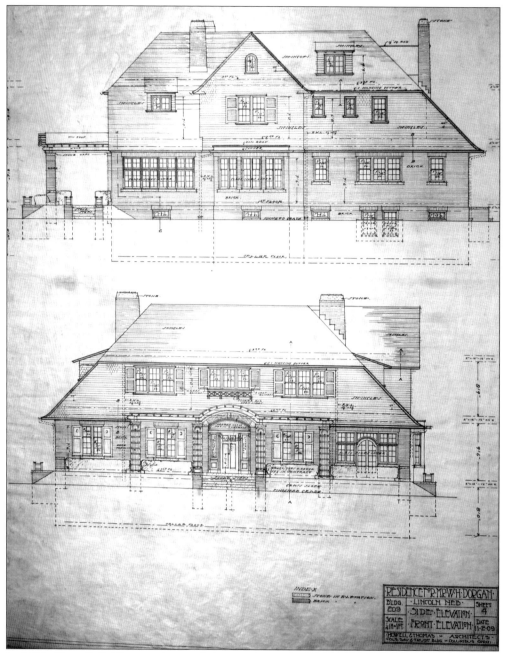

In 1909, Howell & Thomas designed this residence for W.H. Dorgan of Lincoln, Nebraska. Howell & Thomas rarely did work outside of Ohio. In a book of prominent Nebraskans, Dorgan is listed as a "Capitalist and Promoter." This beautiful ink on linen drawing features the front and side elevations. (Cleveland Public Library.)

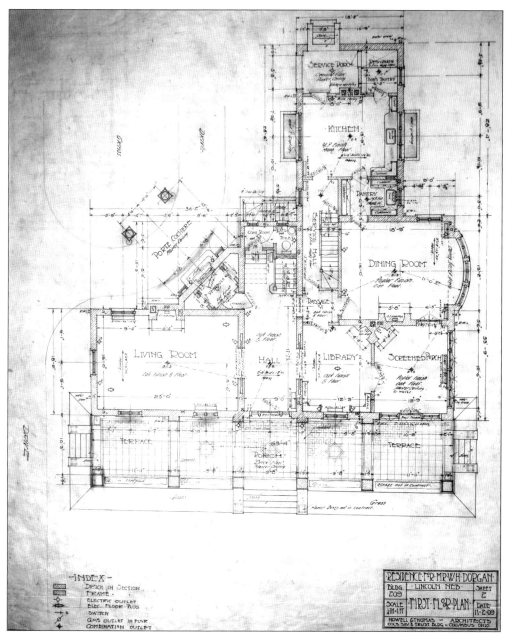

The plan of the first floor of W.H. Dorgan's residence in Lincoln, Nebraska, shows a paved terrace at the front of the house, and a porte cochere leading to the rear entrance. A service wing that incorporates the large (for the time) kitchen is at the rear of the house. (Cleveland Public Library.)

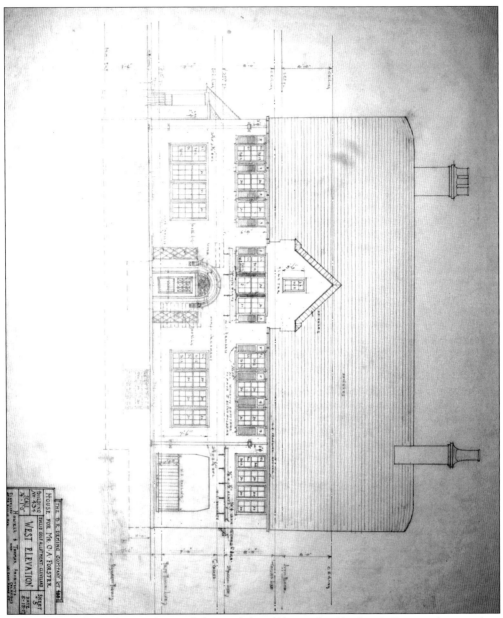

In 1919, Howell & Thomas designed this Euclid Golf house for Charles A. Forster, the president of the Packard Cleveland Motor Company, distributors of Packard automobiles. Located at 2231 Delamere Drive, the dramatic stucco house was built by Deming. (Cleveland Public Library.)

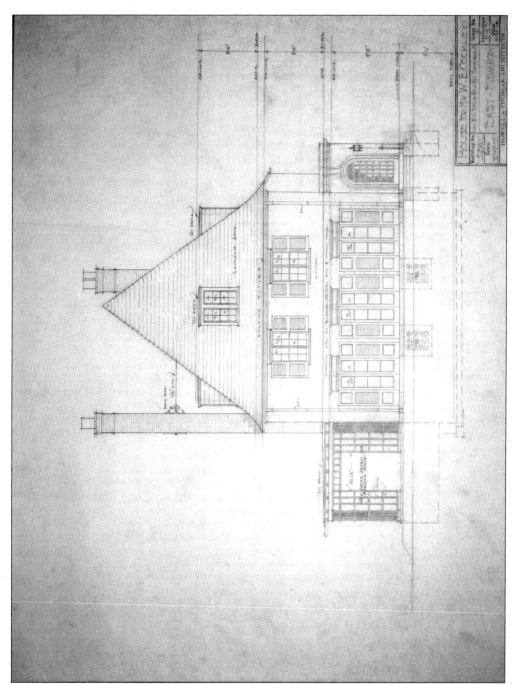

2220 Woodmere Drive was designed by Howell & Thomas for William B. Cockley, a lawyer with the firm Tolles, Hogsett & Ginn. This French inspired house, built in 1918, is finished in stucco with French doors on the first storey and a steeply pitched hipped roof with flared eves. The entrance is on the right side of the house, and a flat roofed sun porch is on the left side. (Cleveland Public Library.)

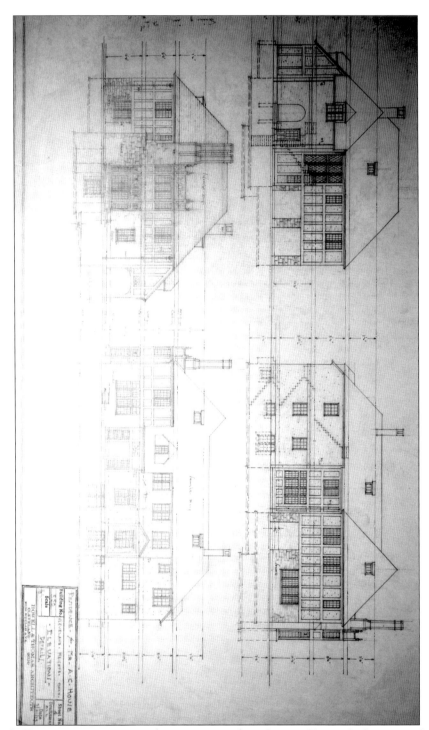

Allan C. House was a partner in the investment firm Curtiss, House & Company. In 1919, House commissioned Howell & Thomas to design a grand, English-inspired residence; however, it was not built. A.C. House would later build a home on Derbyshire Road in Cleveland Heights designed by architect Abram Garfield. (Cleveland Public Library.)

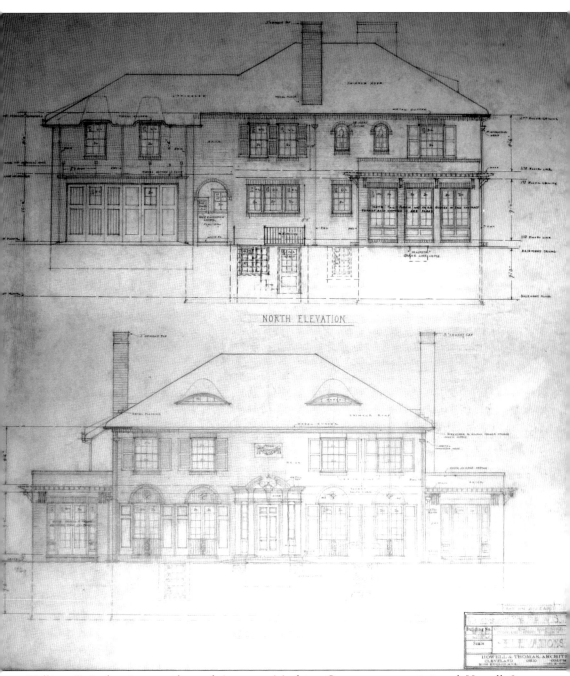

NORTH ELEVATION

William S. Jack, vice president of Accurate Machine Company, commissioned Howell & Thomas to design this Georgian inspired residence at 2325 Delamere Drive in Euclid Golf. The design features symmetrical wings, blind arches in brick over the first storey windows, and a broken pediment over the door. The house was built in 1919. (Cleveland Public Library.)

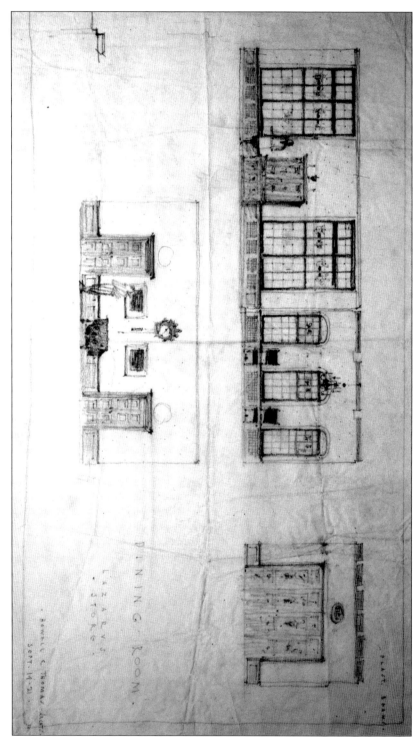

Howell & Thomas designed the façade of the F&R Lazarus department store in Columbus, Ohio, in 1921. The firm also created interiors for Lazarus, including this elevation of the interior of the Tea Room at the top of the store. (Cleveland Public Library.)

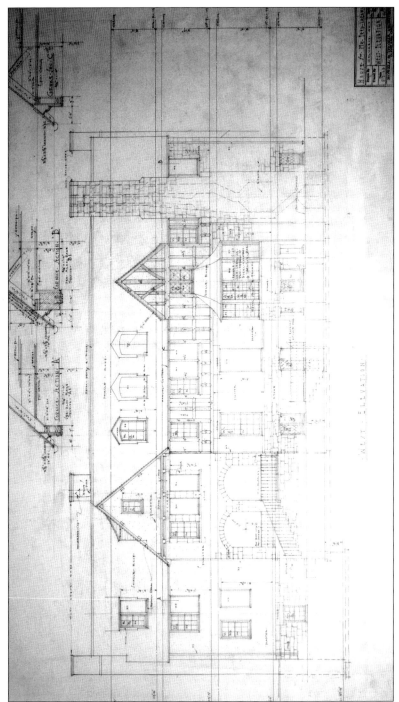

In addition to creating designs for his business, department store president Fred Lazarus Jr. had Howell & Thomas design this grand, English-inspired mansion located at 110 Park Drive in Bexley, Ohio. Fred Lazarus is credited with convincing President Franklin Roosevelt to change the Thanksgiving holiday from the last Thursday of November to the fourth Thursday, extending the Christmas shopping season! (Cleveland Public Library.)

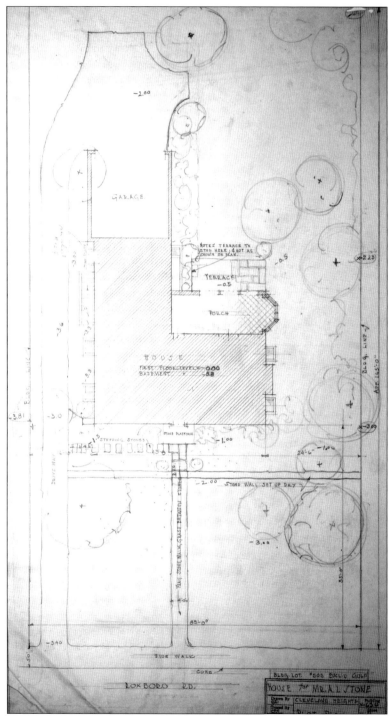

Howell & Thomas also provided clients with landscape designs, as is evident here in this plot plan for the residence of Arthur L. Stone at 2341 Roxboro Road in Euclid Golf. Stone was the treasurer of Northern Ohio Lumber & Timber Company. Deming built Stone's house in 1922. (Cleveland Public Library.)

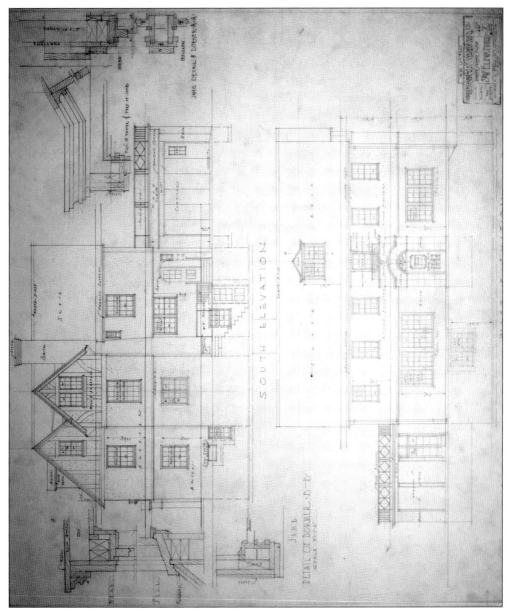

Howell & Thomas designed many model houses at the request of the Van Sweringens of Shaker Heights. One of them is this at 2833 Courtland Boulevard. The original owner of this house was H. Ross Sullivan, purchasing agent and building manager for Central United National Bank. (Cleveland Public Library.)

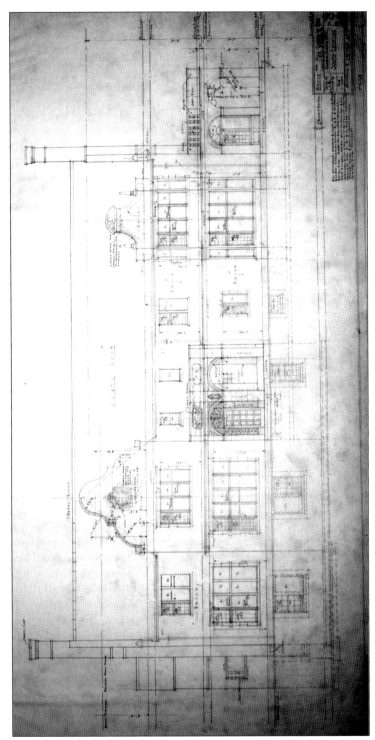

In addition to designing houses for the Van Sweringens, Howell & Thomas designed many houses for individual customers who intended to build in Shaker Heights. One such house is this at 18401 Shaker Boulevard, designed for George W. Hale. (Cleveland Public Library.)

# BIBLIOGRAPHY

B.R. Deming Company. *Euclid Golf Allotment.* Cleveland: The B.R. Deming Company, 1914.
____. *Euclid Golf Neighborhood.* Columbus: Denny A. Clark, 1920.
____.Advertisement, *Cleveland Leader,* 1 June 1913, real estate section.
Borchert, James. "Downtown, Uptown, Out of Town: Diverging Patterns of Upper Class Residential Landscapes in Buffalo, Pittsburgh and Cleveland 1885-1935." Cleveland.
____."From City to Suburb: The Strange Case of Cleveland's Disappearing Elite and Their Changing Residential Landscapes: 1885–1935." Proceedings of the Ohio Academy of History, Marion, Ohio, 2000.
Campen, Richard N. *Distinguished Homes of Shaker Heights.* Fort Myers, Florida: West Summit Press, 1992.
Cleveland Directory Company. *Cleveland City Directory,* 1916–1935.
*Cleveland Heights Dispatch, The,* 1920s.
*Cleveland Leader, The,* 1913–1929.
Cleveland Topics Company. *Cleveland Town Topics,* 1913–1929.
"Colonial Type Sets Pace for Building On New Lots," *Cleveland Leader,* 8 June 1913, real estate section.
Haberman, Ian. *The Van Sweringens of Cleveland: The Biography of an Empire.* Cleveland: The Western Reserve Historical Society, 1979.
Hayes, Blaine S. and James A. Toman. *Horse Trails to Regional Rails: The Story of Public Transit in Greater Cleveland.* Kent, Ohio: The Kent State University Press, 1996.
"Homes and Homesites at the Heights Where Busiest Season is Expected," *Cleveland Leader,* 6 April 1913, real estate section.
"House of B.R. Deming, Esq., Cleveland Ohio," *Architectural Forum* 26, May 1917, 126–127.
Johannesen, Eric. *Cleveland Architecture 1876–1976.* Cleveland: Western Reserve Historical Society, 1979.
Mayfield Country Club. *Mayfield Country Club on its 75th Anniversary, The,* pamphlet, 1986.
McAlester, Virginia and Lee. *A Field Guide to American Houses.* New York: Alfred A. Knopf, Inc., 1996.
Morton, Marian. *Cleveland Heights, Ohio: The Making of an Urban Suburb, 1847–2002.* Charleston: Arcadia Publishing, 2002.
Obituary of B.R. Deming, *Cleveland Plain Dealer,* 15 December 15 1956, obituaries.
*Ohio Architect, Engineer and Builder, The,* 1904–1919.
"Opening of Euclid Golf Allotment," *Cleveland Leader,* 11 May 1913, real estate section.
"One Visit to Euclid Golf Allotment Will Make You Want to Build Your Home There," *Cleveland Leader,* 18 May 1913, real estate section.
Orth, Samuel Peter. *A History of Cleveland Ohio, Vol. 2.* Chicago and Cleveland: S.J. Clarke Publishing Company, 1910.
*Plain Dealer, The,* 1913–1929.
*Representative Clevelanders.* Cleveland: The Cleveland Topics Company, 1927.
Seagrave, Alice D., Comp. and Ed. *Golf Retold: The Story of Golf in Cleveland.* Cleveland: The Cleveland Women's Golf Association, 1940.
*Shaker Heights Ideal Home Sites.* Cleveland: C.C. Ringle & Company, 1904.

*The Shaker Heights Land Company Subdivision.* Cleveland: F.A. Pease Engineering Company, February 1904.

Smith, Howard Dwight. "'Euclid Golf,' Cleveland Ohio," *Architectural Forum*, May 1921, 165–172.

## ARCHIVAL SOURCES

Abeyton Realty Company. Correspondence with Grant Deming and the B.R. Deming Company, 1909–1924. Rockefeller Archives, Sleepy Hollow, NY.

Abeyton Realty Company and Barton R. Deming. Memorandum of Agreement, June 1915. Rockefeller Archives, Sleepy Hollow, NY.

Abeyton Realty Company. Mortgage Deed transferring ownership of Euclid Golf to Barton R. Deming Company, October 3, 1919. Rockefeller Archives, Sleepy Hollow, NY.

Bremer, Deanna L. and Hugh P. Fisher. Nomination of Euclid Golf Neighborhood. National Register of Historic Places, Washington, D.C., April 2002.

City of Cleveland Heights, City Hall. Record of Building Permits. Cleveland Heights, Ohio.

Deming Jr., Grant W., interview by Deanna L. Bremer, written interview, Cleveland, Ohio, October, 2000.

Johannesen, Eric and Derek Ostergard. Nomination of Fairmount Boulevard Historic District. National Register of Historic Places, Washington, D.C., October 1976.

Warranty Deed for property of M.L. Hopkins at 2334 Roxboro Road, January 1918. Cleveland Heights, Ohio.